"I have had the privilege of working with Chr[i]
integrate the Needs Led Assessment Programme i
care. This framework has deepened our insight and understanding of unmet needs and destructive behaviours and equipped us with the necessary tools to reach their inner world and guide them on a therapeutic journey towards self-discovery and healing. This manual and the previous book provide an essential guide to policy makers, service providers and practitioners who are dedicated to making a lasting difference to the lives of children who have endured trauma and adversity."

Amanda Knowles MBE, *Services to residential childcare, director Mulberry Care and Future Horizons Support Services (for care leavers)*

"Christine started her career at the Cotswold Community, a pioneering therapeutic community home for children profoundly affected by early trauma, working alongside Barbara Dockar Drydale who built on the pioneering work of Donald Winnicott. Christine's work on Needs Led Assessment and Treatment Plans stems from those early days, and whilst maintaining the underlying philosophy, has evolved into a manual to be used by staff and carers who wish to work therapeutically with children and young people whose early life experiences have been significantly affected by trauma."

Mark Thomas, *head of service, ALL4U Fostering*

"As CEO of The Caldecott Foundation, I was thrilled to have Christine work along-side our managers and carers developing Needs Led Assessments and Therapeutic Treatment Programmes for children and young people who have experienced pro-found trauma. Her guidance has helped the team to respond, not react to behaviours presented. In-depth mentalisation, discussion and reflective practice has enabled them to understand that this is a journey, not a quick fix, and has provided hope for children and adults working alongside them in therapeutic care. This manual offers invaluable insight into the impact of childhood trauma and shows how we can reach the inner child."

Nick Barnett, *CEO The Caldicott Foundation*

"The authors provide a 'back to the source' book for workers and carers working directly with profoundly traumatised children and young people. They communi-cate the tools for thinking and planning for today's practitioners to use in the service of children's recovery from trauma. This manual is for all those who consider children's needs are becoming more challenging, providing essential experienced based-practice reaching back to the foundation of psychosocial Residential Thera-peutic Child Care. The results of their collective creative responses are here, refined treasures from a continuing tradition. This really works!"

Jonathan Stanley, *principal partner, National Centre of Excellence for Residential Child Care (NCERCC)*

Developing a Therapeutic Treatment Programme for Traumatised Children and Young People

This manual sets out an accessible model for assessing the emotional needs of traumatised children and young adults and using the outcomes of the assessment to develop individualised therapeutic programmes to support their needs and emotional development.

Evolved from Christine Bradley's experience of over 40 years of working with children and young people with complex histories, the model and the case studies presented are firmly rooted in a psychotherapeutic approach and her early training of working with pioneers in the field. It presents a Needs Led Assessment and Therapeutic Treatment model that offers insight and an understanding of the complex histories and behaviours of individual children and young people based on the impact that trauma has on the inner world of the child. The treatment programme is presented in a clearly written and highly accessible step-by-step approach that is supplemented by exemplar case studies and moving anecdotes.

This manual will be of use to any professional working with traumatised children and young people including therapists, social workers, foster carers, and teachers. It will allow individuals who otherwise would not feel they possess the confidence, knowledge, training, or experience to carry out a detailed and effective Needs Led Assessment followed by a Therapeutic Treatment Programme that is tailored to the specific needs of the child or young person.

Christine Bradley is an experienced practitioner and author who has worked with vulnerable children for over 40 years. She began her career at the Cotswold Community, then became a senior officer for the London borough of Wandsworth and director of the Caldecott College in Kent. She is a consultant, nationally and internationally, for organisations in residential care, therapeutic communities, and adoption/fostering agencies.

Francia Kinchington is an education leadership and development consultant, author, and editor with extensive international experience. Formally a principal lecturer at the University of Greenwich for 25 years, she is an experienced doctoral supervisor and examiner and a graduate member of the British Psychological Society.

Developing a Therapeutic Treatment Programme for Traumatised Children and Young People

A Needs Led Assessment Model

Christine Bradley with Francia Kinchington

Routledge
Taylor & Francis Group

LONDON AND NEW YORK

Designed cover image: © Maple House Residential Children's Home

First published 2025
by Routledge
4 Park Square, Milton Park, Abingdon, Oxon OX14 4RN

and by Routledge
605 Third Avenue, New York, NY 10158

Routledge is an imprint of the Taylor & Francis Group, an informa business

© 2025 Christine Bradley with Francia Kinchington

British Library Cataloguing-in-Publication Data
A catalogue record for this book is available from the British Library

ISBN: 978-1-032-65757-8 (hbk)
ISBN: 978-1-032-65756-1 (pbk)
ISBN: 978-1-032-65759-2 (ebk)

DOI: 10.4324/9781032657592

Typeset in Times New Roman
by KnowledgeWorks Global Ltd.

Contents

Introducing a new model for assessing and treating children and young people who have experienced and lived with the legacy of early trauma

Christine Bradley

The manual is aimed specifically at carers and workers who work with traumatised children and young people in therapeutic contexts and are directly involved in their assessment and the planning of appropriate therapeutic treatment. The terms 'carers' and 'workers' are used as short-hand terms to apply to the wide range of individuals involved in caring, working, and living alongside this group of children and young people with complex needs. These will range from foster carers, both short and long term, kinship carers, adoptive parents, teachers, carers, and health workers who work in special school settings for children and young people who are autistic, mentally or physically disabled, teachers who work with children on the special educational needs and disabilities (SEND) register or in pupil referral units, carers who work with families where either the child's parent or main carer has health or mental health issues, workers who work with unaccompanied asylum-seeking children, to staff in residential children's homes and secure units.

Children and young people who have been through early trauma differ profoundly from children who have experienced emotionally secure early bonding and attachment relationships with their primary carers. However, with appropriate support, children and young people can work through the fears and anxieties which they have internalised, to reach a point where they are more able to think about their painful feelings. The impact of trauma on a child or young person who did not develop a meaningful and secure attachment relationship with their primary carer and was subjected to reactions of emotional abandonment, hostility, constant abuse, and trauma is overwhelming. This experience is debilitating and results in the child becoming emotionally fragmented, unable to bring together the different aspects of how they feel about themselves, and leaving them unable to integrate further experiences and manage the painful realities of their day-to-day living. They expect the trauma of their earlier years to be repeated, a pattern characterised by anticipated on-going hostility and aggression from others. Without appropriate help and therapeutic treatment, they can view the outside world (reality) as being there to attack them, which they respond to by attacking back. Their behaviour is characterised by a failure to conform to social norms, a lack of remorse, and little

DOI: 10.4324/9781032657592-1

sense of being able to accept personal responsibility for their actions. The long-term outcome for these children can be poor, both educationally and socially, with the incidence of depression increasingly markedly over the last few years (Trowell and Miles, 2011: 34).

The model for Needs Led Assessment and Therapeutic Treatment Plans used with children and young people, who have experienced early trauma and as a result have complex emotional and behavioural needs, has evolved from its original therapeutic roots and developed into the model presented in this manual. It offers an individualised approach, a way forward for children and young people who are locked into experiences and overwhelming emotions which neither they or their workers are able to move beyond, to grow emotionally, developing their ability to manage the pressures of external reality without breaking down.

The model has been used in practice, developed, and evolved over a number of years and has been found to provide effective guidance, which enables workers to acquire the insight and understanding needed to work effectively with these children and young people. The model, content, and guidance presented in the manual are grounded in a psychotherapeutic understanding that has evolved over a 40-year period of working with children and young people with complex histories and behaviours within care settings. It is rooted in Christine Bradley's early experience of working with and guided by Barbara Dockar-Drysdale (consultant psychotherapist and founder of the Mulberry Bush School, Oxford) and Richard Balbernie (principal of the Cotswold Community), who were both inspired by and worked with Dr. Donald Winnicott, a pioneering child psychoanalyst. Their work with emotionally damaged children and young people was developed and tested out in the work of the Cotswold Community School in Wiltshire and subsequently extended by Christine Bradley through her work as a consultant with local authorities, and a wide range of residential childcare settings, nationally and internationally, over the past four decades. Although the Cotswold Community had originally been an approved school for young offenders, it eventually transformed into a successful therapeutic community working with young offenders who had often failed in other placements. The impact of their innovative practice using Needs Led Assessment and Therapeutic Treatment Programmes was that after 10 years, they were able to show that recidivism (young people returning to young offenders' units or prisons) had dropped from a previous 85% when it was a formal approved school to 0.5% after it changed to becoming a therapeutic community focusing on recognising and meeting the emotional needs of the children and young people in their care.

The aim of the assessment was to identify the level of privation and deprivation, today known as trauma, and the impact these experiences had on the child's developing self, and also to understand how such experiences prevented their **sense of self** from developing. Unintegration is recognised as a pre-attachment syndrome, and it was recognised that unintegrated children, without appropriate therapeutic provision and support would remain emotionally stuck at a more primitive level of emotional development, in danger of acting out their emotions of panic and rage which remain held within them becoming destructive or self-destructive.

The main task of the Needs Led Assessment is not to label or diagnose the child or young person's difficulties but to identify the fragmented aspects of their emotions and understand how they could be helped to manage the reality factors of their day-to-day living. A treatment plan is designed to help carers and workers to create a positive and therapeutic response to the child or young person's behaviour by creating a therapeutic treatment programme, which provides strategies for the appropriate provision and support to be put into place enabling the child or young person to grow emotionally. The process enables carers and workers to develop sufficient insight and understanding about the meaning of their behaviour and enables the child or young person to believe that they are being understood and listened to by the carer or worker with meaning and sincerity.

The importance of the Needs Led Assessment and Therapeutic Treatment Programme is that it is tailored to the individual child or young person, helping to identify the specific aspects of their emotional development which, because of their early trauma, has left them fixed at an infantile of early childhood stage of development, preventing them from functioning in an age-appropriate way. The process of carrying out a Needs Led Assessment and Therapeutic Treatment Plan enables workers to reach out to the unbearable feelings of hopelessness and helplessness that the child or young person carries within them and respond appropriately. The task is to work towards reaching a positive outcome for the traumatised child or young person, enabling them to find a point at which they become more able to manage the challenges of external reality without breaking down, and move towards becoming more integrated as a person with a stronger sense of self and psychological development.

Since 2015, the current Needs Led Assessment and Therapeutic Treatment Programme model presented in this manual has evolved to define a route through which workers and carers help children and young people whose trauma has left them emotionally frozen, unable to cope with life or make healthy relationships with others. Critically, because these children and young people remain emotionally vulnerable, they are more susceptible to anti-social behaviour and delinquent tendencies.

Although the original format of the Needs Led Assessment and Therapeutic Treatment Programme has been adapted to fit in with the current needs and demands of work with traumatised children and young people, the underlying philosophical underpinning of the work has not been lost and continues to provide the 'heart of the matter' and the basis for insight and understanding by practitioners who provide therapeutic treatment to emotionally fragmented children and young people.

Chapter 2 presents a clear summary defining key terms and concepts used within the book. A familiarity and understanding of key terms enable carers and workers to increase their understanding of how trauma impacts the child or young person's sense of self, their behaviour, relationships with others, and the strategies and behaviours they put into place to manage the outside world. Importantly this understanding enables teams to discuss the behaviours of children and young people in terms of a common language and shared understanding.

Chapter 3 presents a detailed outline of the structure of the revised model comprising the Needs Led Assessment, Therapeutic Treatment Plan, and the workers/carers reflective log. It enables the carer and worker to follow the key processes involved so that they are able to apply these with confidence to the workplace. Key questions are asked, the responses to which enable the team working therapeutically with the unintegrated child or young person to assess their potential categorisation in terms of key classifications comprising frozen, fragmented/archipelago, parentified/carer, and fragile integration. This offers a starting point for developing strategies for therapeutic intervention to support the development of the child or young person.

Chapter 4 presents detailed case studies that include both the new and original models. The new model is presented in three parts comprising an initial Needs Led Assessment and Therapeutic Treatment Plan, the worker/carer's reflective log, and the follow-up Needs Led Assessment and Therapeutic Treatment Plan three months later, enabling the reader to identify the degree to which the child or young person has progressed. The case studies that follow the original model include a final paragraph that discusses the child/young person's current status.

Chapter 5 discusses the impact of profound trauma on the child or young person and reflects on the long-term impact of trauma on the quality of their adolescence, adult life, self-perception, relationships, mental health, and life chances.

Chapter 6 examines the key role played by carers and workers who live alongside and work closely with children and young people who have experienced profound trauma and offers a range of reflective processes which enable carers and workers to manage themselves psychologically in a potentially difficult and stressful environment without succumbing to burnout.

Chapter 7 draws together key strands from each of the preceding chapters to offer guidance and a way forward.

The Afterword, presented by Dr. Judith Trowell, reflects on the importance of the manual in the context of her professional experience as a psychiatrist working with children and adolescents who have experienced sexual abuse, childhood depression, and trauma.

I hope the guidance provided in the manual helps you to work with greater insight and confidence, and to use the Needs Led Assessment and Therapeutic Treatment programmes to support the emotional growth of the children and young people in your care.

Chapter 2

Understanding the vocabulary of working with children and young people who have experienced profound trauma

Francia Kinchington

This chapter defines key terms, enabling carers and workers to familiarise themselves with the definitions, underpinning theory, and concepts that are used in the chapters that follow. Understanding and discussing these terms with colleagues helps to develop not only insight and a deeper understanding of how these relate to the children and young people for whom they are responsible but also to reflect on the impact on themselves as carers and workers living alongside profoundly traumatised children and young people. It is important to set this in context: NICE (2021: 6) reported 80,080 looked-after children and young people in England, of whom 65% entered into the care system mainly because of abuse or neglect. The trauma experienced, which ranges from domestic abuse, serious harm, neglect, sexual, emotional, and physical abuse, to exposure to alcohol and drug misuse in the home or community, has a direct impact on the child or young person's, physical, emotional, and mental health and the capacity for emotional and stress regulation, and self-control. The rate of mental health disorders for children aged 5–15 who are looked after is 45%, and 72% for those in residential care, in comparison to 10% in the general population.

A

Attachment disorders

The majority of traumas met with in general professional practice according to Farnfield and Stokowy (2014: 65) are attachment-based; they stem from actual abuse as in physical, sexual, and emotional abuse, in which the trauma was either caused by attachment figures or carers, or by attachment figures or carers who failed to care and protect the child through neglect.

There are essentially two forms of attachment: secure and insecure.

Secure attachment: Bowlby (1969) suggests that where infants receive care that is attuned to their needs and are confident their cries of hunger, fear, and emotional and physical security are noticed and responded to consistently, they are

DOI: 10.4324/9781032657592-2

described as having a **'secure' attachment**. In contrast, children who receive inconsistent care and where their caregiver is not attuned to their needs are described as having an 'insecure' attachment.

Insecure attachment develops where a child has learnt that they cannot rely on their caregiver to be available and responsive when they are alarmed or distressed. Insecure attachment is **relationship-specific**: a child can have an insecure attachment relationship with one caregiver and a secure attachment relationship with another. Insecure attachment patterns are not fixed traits of the child and attachment status can improve over time where a long-term, stable, and supportive relationship is present of at least a year in length. A change is more likely to occur where the child is placed in a supportive foster family environment, a therapeutic residential setting, or, although more difficult to change, in adulthood through therapy or a secure and supportive marriage. Other adult relationships are unlikely to achieve this change as they lack the essential sustained depth or longevity needed.

Insecure attachment comprises the following:

Anxious attachment occurs where the infant does not feel secure in their relationship with their primary carer and is confused by their inconsistent and unpredictable behaviours. Inconsistent parenting behaviours may be nurturing and attuned at times, but insensitive, emotionally unavailable, or cold and critical, at other times, or may be slow or inconsistent in responding to signs of distress in their baby. As a consequence, the infant and later the young child may cling to their carer, becoming really upset when they leave, and even when they return. This attachment style can increase the risk of anxiety disorders and low self-esteem later in life and have a negative impact on relationships.

Dismissive-avoidant attachment develops where the infant is emotionally neglected by their primary carer who may be unable to attune and care for the infant or show affection or provide good primary provision for the infant. The primary carer may be physically or emotionally unavailable, for example, through depression or mental illness. This attachment style can result in the child being unable to think about their own deeper emotions and feelings, be emotionally distant towards others, and have difficulty in forming close intimate relationships in adult life.

Disorganised attachment is the most extreme form of insecure attachment experienced by the infant. It is thought to emerge from fear where their primary carer is also the one who is abusing them and the source of fear and danger from which they are unable to escape. The infant is frightened when being abused, or feeling frightened by the rage and hatred they are confronted with in the face of the carer. Consequently, the child can be anxiously attached but at the same time experiencing disorganised attachment, or be dismissively attached and disorganised. It can result in social and emotional insecurity and as an adult, an inability to form close intimate relationships.

Reactive attachment disorder (RAD) is a psychiatric diagnosis where the child shows a persistent lack of care-seeking behaviour towards **any** caregivers, even when upset, sick, or scared. If the child feels abandoned, powerless, or neglected, they learn that they cannot depend on others and that the world is a dangerous and hostile place. The lack of reaction by the child towards the caregiver may be apparent at partings and reunions with the caregiver (American Psychiatric Association (APA), 2013; NICE, 2016). The child may also present as extremely withdrawn, emotionally detached, and resistant to comforting.

Disinhibited social engagement disorder (DSED)/disinhibited attachment disorder (DAD) was originally considered as a subtype of **RAD** but is now categorised as a separate disorder (American Psychiatric Association (APA), 2022) by the American Psychiatric Association. DAD/DSED is characterised by strong over-familiarity towards adults that they do not know, and that is out of keeping with age-appropriate boundaries or cultural norms. An example may be that the child could seek to go off with a stranger without checking with caregivers, talking with strangers, or seeking physical comfort, such as hugs, from a person who is not their parent or caregiver, or even wander off with a person they just met. The roots of this disorder lie in disruptions in early attachment particularly where the parent/primary caregiver is absent, abusive, neglectful, or unwilling or unable to offer emotional support. The infant/child learns to recognise that the parent/primary caregiver is not emotionally available to them and does not see a distinction between parents and strangers.

B

Behavioural disorders

Oppositional defiant disorder (ODD) is a disruptive behaviour disorder (DBD) of childhood and adolescence characterised by functional and social impairment and occurs when a child experiences early and profound trauma. The neural pathways in critical parts of the brain such as the prefrontal cortex may either not form or are damaged, preventing messages in the brain from being transmitted. The outcome in children and young people is of recurrent, persistent, developmentally inappropriate patterns of anger, irritability, negativity, defiance, disobedience, and deliberate hostility towards others. Additionally, they will experience dysregulated emotions including temper tantrums, intense fears, inconsolable despair, an inability or difficulty in feeling and expressing emotions, and a low tolerance to frustration co-occurring with externalising behaviour problems, all elements which will be exacerbated during puberty. In these children and young people, emotions seem uncontrollable or absent and they tend to think simplistically, rigidly, and reactively where their interactions are viewed through defiance and aggression.

Conduct disorder (CD) is a behavioural and emotional disorder characterised by poor emotional engagement with little care for others, evidencing deliberate violations of the rights of others, societal norms, or rules. Children with CD typically show aggressive, antisocial behaviour and callous-unemotional (CU) traits, do not take any responsibility for their actions, and show a lack of guilt, physiological under-arousal, and lack of empathy (Paulus et al., 2021: 10).

C

Communication

Non-verbal communication

Non-verbal communication can involve eye contact, gestures, facial expressions, touch, body language, and the use of play objects such as dolls and toys to communicate feelings, wishes, or memories. Non-verbal communication can be used to emphasise or contradict what a child says verbally, so it is an important indicator of emotions and their feelings towards other people (Argyle, 1988). Additionally, non-verbal communication can take the form of signing languages such as British Sign Language (BSL), and communication systems such as Makaton, which use signs and symbols to communicate and are used with young children having autism or learning disabilities.

Symbolic communication

Symbolic communication is a powerful form of communication which the child can use to express emotions which they cannot articulate through words. Individual and shared play, telling stories, creating, and acting in made-up scenarios and plays, using puppets for storytelling, Lego blocks, singing and music, painting and other creative activities offer the child or young person an opportunity to express their emotions, the way they see themselves, their inner world, and their understanding of the world and people outside of themselves. Melanie Klein (1932, 1961) noted that children's play and the way that toys were used carried important and symbolic meaning and this could be analysed and interpreted to provide insight into a child's anxieties, fears, and the painful reality that they carried with them. Symbolic communication can also, for example, be expressed in destructive and self-destructive behaviours. Workers and carers need the skills to recognise and interpret what the child/young person is trying to communicate symbolically and to support the child/young person to understand what they are trying to express emotionally and physically.

Verbal communication

Verbal communication is oral communication involving speaking, listening, and understanding, humour, and encompasses interpersonal communication (talking to another person or to others within a group) and intra-personal communication (talking to oneself, for example, in trying to work something out). Verbal communication enables the child or young person to explain and share their ideas and thoughts with others, to build relationships through finding other young people with whom they have common interests, and where the young person's ideas, understanding of the world, and learning can be extended through forms that carry symbolic meaning such as through reading stories, myths, poetry, and singing.

D

Defence mechanisms

Defence mechanisms are primitive adaptive and maladaptive strategies that evolve when an infant has experienced extreme trauma. These enable the infant to reduce internal stress and to survive in the hostile environment in which they live (Freud, 1937) but inevitably continue into childhood and adulthood and constrain the capacity for social relationships, creativity, personal growth, and development of the self.

Di Giuseppe and Perry (2021) identify **three categories of defensive categories:** mature defences (most adaptive), neurotic, and immature (least adaptive), each of which includes a number of levels that are expressed through a range of individual defences. The three categories comprise:

- Mature defence category can include the use of humour, altruism, suppression, sublimation, identification, and self-assertion to cope with anxiety.
- Neurotic defence category can include the use of intellectualisation, repression, disassociation, reaction formation, and displacement.
- Immature defence category is primitive and the least adaptive of defence levels where the individual defences are expressed through projection, acting out, and splitting of self-image. These defences impact on children and young people's behaviour, the way they perceive themselves and their sense of self, and their relationships and interactions with other people.

Individual defences from the **immature defence category** and intermediate **neurotic defence category** are detailed here, to provide an understanding into the defences, behaviour, and reactions of young children and people who have experienced profound trauma.

Immature depressive defence category comprises four levels

The immature defensive category (Levels 1 and 2) is centred on physical action and is the most extensive of all defences. Action defences enable the child to view the stress or conflict as being external, leading them to explosive action externally (on others or their environment) or themselves, releasing tension, gratifying wishes, and/or avoiding fears, but without anticipating the negative consequences. This avoids the child having to 'own' the unbearable emotions that arise from within themselves.

Level 1 is centred on action: acting out, passive aggression, help-rejecting complaining.

- **Acting out:** where the child or young person cannot cope with their internal anxiety and emotional chaos, or external stressors in their life and expresses this through uncontrolled behaviour without regard to the consequence either for themselves or other people and may be self-destructive or socially disruptive. It usually occurs in response to interpersonal interactions or events with significant people in the child or young person's life, such as parents, authority figures, and friends.
- **Passive aggression:** where the child deals with internal and external emotional stress and conflicts through the passive expression of anger and resentment towards another person, but in extreme cases can be turned in on themselves, e.g., by being stubborn, inept, procrastinating, never finishing things, or being forgetful. The child feels powerless and resentful and has learnt to expect punishment, frustration, or their needs dismissed if they show their feelings or needs to someone who has power over them.
- **Help-rejecting complaining:** where the child constantly complains that 'people don't care' even though they have tried very hard to help.

Level 2: major image-distorting defences comprise **splitting** (self-image and splitting of other's image) and **identification with the abuser**. These defences protect the child from intolerable anxiety when faced with having to think about or accept a parent or carer's abuse.

- **Splitting** enables the child to deal with extreme emotional conflict, whether internal or external, by defaulting to 'all good' or 'all bad' world view. They are unable to integrate both aspects within a single person whether themselves or other people, e.g., their carer. Splitting of self-images often occurs alongside splitting of others' images, since they both were learned in response to the unpredictability of one's primary carer. Splitting is a defence against the anxiety of ruining the 'good' or idealised image of, e.g., a parent or carer by allowing the bad aspects of them to intrude. The child cannot hold onto contradictions of both fearing and hating whilst loving and depending on their primary carer, at the same time. Additionally, the child/young person misreads and misinterprets cues from others and views them as reflections of their inner feelings, for example, *"he gave me a nasty look, so I know he hates me" or "I feel so bad that I know you must hate me, so why should I trust up to you?"*. The capacity to bring these contradictory feelings and perceptions together, to reconcile the split, only occurs through therapeutic intervention and the development of 'Integration'.

- **Identification with the abuser** is the defence of the traumatised child who believes that **they** (not the abuser) were responsible for the trauma that they experienced and that it was their own fault that it occurred. The emotional attachment of victims of intimidation and abuse towards their abuser is really a survival strategy where the weak identify with the powerful (Freud, 1937). The defence is then triggered when the child feels threatened (real or imagined) and consequently feels justified in attacking in response. The child's interpretation is that it was the other person who deliberately made them feel angry or scared, so their emotional response, for example, anger or fear, was justified.

Level 3: disavowal defence level comprises:

- Projection is where the child or young person unconsciously attributes unwanted emotions or traits which they cannot accept about themselves, onto another person such as a parent or teacher, or a group of people such as the children in their class, so that their thinking becomes "they are angry with me because they hate me".
- Denial is used to avoid dealing with a stressful or overwhelming situation. When a child or young person is in denial, they refuse to accept the reality of their situation. Remaining in a state of denial will disconnect a child/young person from reality.
- Rationalisation is used to justify or explain away an unacceptable or uncomfortable feeling, e.g., guilt or embarrassment or event, with an apparently reasonable explanation in order to reduce the feeling, whilst failing to acknowledge the real reason for that feeling.
- Autistic fantasy involves the child daydreaming or retreating into a fantasy world that replaces real social interactions and relationships, using this as a way of alleviating the stress and anxiety in their day-to-day life.

Level 4: minor image-distorting defences comprise:

- Idealisation of self-image or other's image: where the child or young person holds an idealised or perfect image of themselves or of other people that they are normally close to that is unrealistic or exaggerated in response to feelings of insecurity, inadequacy, or powerlessness.
- Devaluation of self-image or other's image occurs when perceptions of themselves or others suddenly collapse because the child or young person is challenged, threatened, or disappointed and they feel intense anger, seeing what they thought of as perfect now as bad or worthless.
- Omnipotence is a distortion of reality where the child holds an idea that they can control or influence their outside world through their thoughts and wishes. Omnipotence is experienced when the infant becomes aware that they can influence their environment in order to have their needs met (cry to get their mother to feed them or change their nappy). However, where the infant's needs are not met consistently, Winnicott proposed that this sense of

omnipotence would not develop, compelling the infant to focus away from meeting their own needs to meeting the needs of their mother. The infant then learns that in order to meet the needs of the mother they have to become who the mother wants them to be. Winnicott theorised that this would lead to the development of the *false self*.

Neurotic defence category comprises

- Repression where the child unconsciously blocks out incidents of trauma and the overwhelming emotions that accompany them so that they disappear from the conscious memory. However, repressed memories or feelings do not simply disappear, they exist 'below the waterline' and may emerge or be triggered, for example, at times of extreme stress or during therapy.
- Dissociation may involve the child mentally separating themselves from their experience of the physical trauma, e.g., sexual abuse, allowing them to feel numb or detached. The child's helplessness, their inability to stop the maltreatment, and their inability to express their emotions may result in dissociating themselves from their experiences of abuse and blaming themselves rather than the perpetrator. The repercussions of the latent physical and emotional trauma can result in experiencing sleep difficulties, a negative self-concept, interpersonal problems, emotional dysregulation, and self-harm (Paulus et al., 2021: 6).
- Reaction formation which involves the child or young person distorting what they really feel which makes them feel anxious or guilty, expressing the opposite of their true feelings, sometimes to an exaggerated extent.
- Displacement which involves taking out difficult feelings, frustrations, and impulses on an object or someone else that is perceived as less threatening. Displacement can also be focused by the child on themselves, where their feelings of anger, hatred, and aggression are turned inwards and expressed as feelings of inferiority, inadequacy, guilt, and depression.

Deprivation versus privation

Deprivation is centred on a loss of emotional or physical care and occurs when a child who has experienced attachment is separated from their primary attachment figure for a period of time.

Privation is centred on 'lack' and occurs when a child has never been able to form an attachment. This is likely to be rooted in an underlying cause of physical, sexual, or emotional abuse, neglect, or institutionalisation, with long-term permanent consequences (Rutter, 1981).

Depression

Depression in children and young people is characterised by feelings of sadness, being upset, a low mood most of the time, feeling irritable, numb, or empty, avoiding friends and social interaction, withdrawing from previously enjoyed activities, sleeping more or less than usual, eating more or less than usual, an inability to concentrate, feeling hopeless, self-critical, lacking energy, feeling guilty, engaging in self-harm, and having thoughts of suicide. It may manifest itself in difficult behaviour in school and drug or alcohol abuse in older children.

Negele et al. (2015) report that there is consensus indicating that childhood trauma is significantly involved in the development of depression. This includes experiencing physical, sexual, or psychological abuse or neglect, witnessing violence or a traumatic event, or having an unstable family environment but can also include experiences of bereavement, parents separating, moving schools, being bullied, and genetic risk factors such as having a parent with a serious mental illness.

Trowell et al. (2007) advocate the value of psychodynamic psychotherapy in being able to bring about more lasting changes in childhood depression by improving the capacity of the child or young person to resolve internal and external conflicts over time. A randomised control trial of 72 children and adolescents aged 9–15 years old with moderate and severe depression showed that they responded very effectively to either individual or family psychodynamic psychotherapy with follow-up results that persisted and showed ongoing improvement. Follow-up, six months after treatment had ended, showed that 100% of cases in the Individual Therapy group and 81% of cases in the Family Therapy group were no longer clinically depressed.

E

Ego and ego functioning

The infant's sense of self and identity (the ego) emerges through the infant's interaction and the attunement of the mother or primary carer. Ego functioning refers to the capacity of the ego (the child's self-awareness) to reflect on their thoughts, feelings, and habits, and either repress them or allow them to be thought about, acted on, and shared with others. The ego has an important function in that it has the capacity to perceive and understand stimuli accurately, to enable the child to recognise and separate their internal world and what is taking place within their mind, with what is occurring in the external world (Winnicott, 2016). A child that experienced early trauma, which has disrupted the development of their self and identity, may be unaware of who they are, lack the insight to understand their own thoughts, feelings, and actions, may have low self-esteem and lack empathy, namely the capacity to understand these elements in others They may unconsciously use defence mechanisms such as denial and repression to repress uncomfortable or traumatising experiences, and may as a result exhibit impulsiveness, and experience a lack of agency feeling that they are controlled by their environment.

Emotional development

Although the potential for emotional development is hardwired into the infant's brain, it evolves through interactions with the primary carer. The infant brain is 'experience-dependent' and develops physically within an interpersonal context, shaped by the nature and quality of early caregiver-infant interactions.

Early postnatal development of brain structures such as the limbic system, which influences emotion, learning, and memory, and hormonal influences, contribute to the activation and regulation of emotion expression. The biological changes that occur are mediated by the emotional and physical sensitivity of the primary caregiver and their responses to the infant's needs and distress. The caregiver may either respond to the infant's needs with sensitivity and soothe them, supporting the development of a secure attachment and socio-emotional competence, or in contrast, in a non-responsive way where the infant learns that their distress and needs will not be met in a predictable way. The infant's emotional responses, in turn, provide feedback to the caregiver, serving to shape their perception of the infant as an 'easy' or 'difficult' baby and, in turn, to shape the infant's developing self-awareness and understanding of the emotional display 'rules' in their environment (Paulus et al., 2021: 2). This begins to shape the relationship between the infant and the carer, and critically, the child's own sense of self.

Emotional dysregulation

Emotional dysregulation occurs where the prefrontal cortex which controls emotional regulation is impaired by extreme trauma during the infant's early development. This affects the growing child's ability to process and control impulses and behaviour, memory, concentration, information and decision-making processing, and their ability to interact socially and is exacerbated where adrenaline and stress hormones flood the body as a result of extreme trauma.

Early disruptions to early caregiver-child relationships according to (Newman et al., 2015: 1), have been found to result in alterations of particular brain regions implicated in emotional regulation. The impact on the emotional capacity of a child or young person who has experienced complex and early trauma is profound, since it arrests emotional functioning. It affects their **emotional awareness** (the ability to recognise and identify one's own and others' emotions); **social competence** (the ability to establish and maintain good relationships with others) and **well-being competencies** (abilities related to the adoption of appropriate and responsible behaviours to effectively deal with the challenges of everyday life); **emotional autonomy** (the set of characteristics and factors related to personal self-management) and **emotional regulation** (the ability to manage and control emotions and responses to them effectively). The inability to exercise emotional autonomy and emotional regulation is a critical factor in the functioning and behaviour of a young person living with profound trauma. The root of the 'malfunctioning' of emotional capacity and responsiveness lies in the child's response to traumatic experiences, where, in order to survive emotionally and physically, the child must inhibit and suppress the outward signs of their inner feelings of fear, anger, and helplessness. Although suppression can control the behavioural response to the trauma (crying, showing fear), it does not change the intensity of the internal emotional experience, but instead changes the way that the experience is remembered, and increases the child's physiological response (Gross, 2002: 281). The response may take the form of rage and anger, physical aggression towards themselves and others, impulsivity, which may take the form of harmful risk-taking behaviours, obsessing about suicide, and extreme moods swings which range from elation to depression.

F

False self

The false self originates with a failure in the interaction between the mother/primary carer and the child and their inability to meet the child's emotional needs (primary maternal preoccupation) or early profound trauma so that the child in order to survive develops a defence mechanism in the form of a false self. This false self presents as real (leading people to think that this is the real child) but is in fact a façade, in which personal relationship and intimacy cannot be sustained, and begins to fail since the true self is hidden. Winnicott writes,

> *The false self has one important function: To hide the true self, which it does by compliance with the environmental demands. In extreme examples of false self- development, the true self is so well hidden that spontaneity is not a feature of their living experiences. Compliance is the main feature with imitation as a speciality.*

> (1965: 147)

The child or young person will function on a superficial level only and can very easily break down to act out displaying overwhelming levels of panic and rage. They are vulnerable to enmeshed attachment (merging) and to destructive and/ or self-destructive outcomes in their life. A child or young person who presents with a false self will need therapeutic support to regress before they can progress healthily.

Fragile integration (disorganised attachment)

Children and young people assessed as having fragile integration (also labelled as disorganised or anxious attachment) live with unresolved trauma and loss. Although the infant or small child formed a rudimentary relationship with a primary carer, the attachment was insufficiently strong or secure enough to enable integration to take place. The result is that since the child is emotionally fragile, their inner world is unable to manage the demands of the external world or resolve issues in their day-to-day lives. Although there is a developing sense of self, it is not yet strong enough to manage stress and anxiety so will disintegrate when the child or young person feels overwhelmed with stress as they are unable to hold onto anxiety and stress without strong support from their carer.

Fragmented/archipelago child

Although the fragmented/archipelago child or young person has had the advantage of some good infantile experiences, a breakdown occurred before they had managed a natural separation from their primary carer. Consequently, they possess areas of functioning which are not sufficiently integrated to create a coherent sense of self, together with areas of non-functioning which are locked into an early infantile state of loss.

It is important that functioning areas are supported, whilst at the same time, non-functioning areas need to be thought through by workers and addressed constructively. Non-functioning areas can give rise to depression and deep despair and can result in a disintegration of self-esteem with the child or young person becoming self-destructive or self-harming. There is an expectation of failure when under stress and a need for a great deal of support to survive their overwhelming sense of loss and fear of abandonment.

Frozen child

The 'frozen self' is emotionally unintegrated and develops as a result of an interruption in the infant's primary experience at the point where the mother/primary carer would be starting the process of separation. Survival mechanisms come into being at this infantile stage of their life, before they had the capacity to think, because their mother/primary carer could not 'hold them in mind'. As a result, the frozen child exists without boundaries to their personality, merges with their environment, and is unable to manage the intimacy of attachment relationships, or to feel the need for them. In order for the frozen child to evolve, the actual emotional experience of 'separating' must occur, so that the child's identity is established, boundaries are defined and accepted, and a state of dependence on a key adult/carer/worker is reached. This will involve containment of self-destructive patterns and behaviours, interruption of any mergers taking place, anticipation of confrontation in advance, and understanding 'acting-out' as a form of communication. The child or young person will disrupt boundaries and find living in their own reality safer than actual reality. Additionally, because the child or young person has very few areas of functioning in their day-to-day living, they are left with gaps which are masked by panic and rage. These lie beneath the surface and emerge under the slighted stress through destructive and self-destructive acting-out behaviours.

H

Holding in mind

A child or young person that needs 'holding in mind' by a carer did not, as an infant, have an attuned mother or primary carer who was able to recognise and 'hold' the infant's emotions and reflect them back in a way that the infant perceived that the carer understood them. As a consequence, the young child does not have a self-containing capacity but needs the individual caring for them to fulfil that function, helping them to recognise and make sense of their feelings. An adult with the responsibility to care for a child or young person in a foster or residential setting needs to 'hear' and respond with sensitivity to the child's unmanageable feelings of fear, hunger, loss, anger, or helplessness, which they project onto the carer. The carer or worker needs to have the capacity to acknowledge the child's anxieties, showing that they have heard and understood the child, and so lessen the burden on the child. Trying to develop the child's own 'containing capacity' becomes an issue for staff where staff experience vicarious trauma and low morale, and where transference and countertransference boundaries have become blurred in their interactions with the children and young adults that they care for on a daily basis.

I

Integration

Integration (Winnicott, 1964, 1965) refers to the process of the emergence of an integrated self within the infant. Initially, pre-birth and at birth, the infant's self is **unintegrated**. At six months, the motor, sensory, and emotional elements of the infant's experience gradually begin the process of coming together in a state described as **disintegration**. At this point, if the infant experiences a secure and attuned relationship with their primary carer, a process of **reintegration** takes place and the infant is said to be in a state of **fragile integration**. Central to the development of integration is the concept of the infant's development of their own self 'containing capacity'. This capacity for self-containment is an unconscious process and, importantly, enables the growing child to reflect and think about how they feel. The young child learns to make sense of the feelings and thoughts, about the predictability (or not) of their environment, their relationships with others, and themselves as an evolving individual. Bion (1962) introduced the idea of the **mother** acting as the initial 'container' for the infant/child's projections, and by responding sensitively and in an empathic way to these, she provides emotional containment, showing the infant/child that they are understood (rather than responding to the infant/child with anger or denying their needs or anxiety), and helping them, in turn, to understand what they are experiencing. This process enables the infant to develop their own containing capacity. Where the child grows up without this, as in the case of profound trauma during infancy, the foster carer or therapeutic residential care worker who is responsible for them will need to fulfil that function by 'holding them in mind', reassuring them that their fears and needs are recognised and addressed.

M

Memory and trauma

Episodic memory refers to long-term memory that involves conscious recollection of previous experiences together with their context in terms of time, place, and associated emotions. Profoundly traumatic experiences may be altered in two ways: physically and psychologically.

Physically, this takes place in the way that the memory of the event has been processed by the brain (in the hippocampus) at the time of the event taking place as a result of the release of, e.g., cortisol, which is released during stressful events and leads to damage of hippocampal neurons. The event experienced, in the form of words, actions, smells, physical and emotional pain, and emotions felt, such as fear, anger, guilt, and powerlessness, together with the sequence of events, become fragmented and confused so that the child is unable to recall the event itself, or may even begin to doubt that the events took place.

The emotional memory of the trauma is processed in the amygdala and, even though suppressed, can be triggered in particular circumstances (e.g. smell, another person's behaviour, aggression, language used, the dark), causing the emotional memories of fear or anxiety and recurring intrusive thoughts to surface. Memory loss of the trauma, together with verbal impairment and sleep disorders, may be indicative of post-traumatic stress, which may have a life-long impact (Petzold and Bunzeck, 2022). Psychologically, memories of the trauma event may be unconsciously or consciously repressed by a child or young person because they are so overwhelming and frightening that they cannot be physically thought or spoken about (*see Defence mechanisms: repression and dissociation*).

Mentalisation refers to the early bonding feedback loop involving visual, auditory, and tactile interaction between the mother/primary carer and infant and is one of the key processes that take place during the process of attachment. This attunement where the carer is centred and attuned to the infant's needs, responses, and behaviour provides an important contribution to the emotional development of the infant. It is during this process that there is an awareness that the infant's inner experiences are recognised and reflected back by the outer world (the carer) and so become anchored in the infants own 'self-state' (Gergely and Watson, 1996). This attunement enables the infant to begin to form their own sense of self as separate from their mother/primary carer on whom they depend for their survival. The process of mentalisation can be disrupted through early maternal/

primary caregiver neglect, maternal/primary caregiver depression, and abuse of the infant. The outcome is a disruption of the emotional and social interaction between the mother/primary caregiver and infant, which is experienced by the infant as stress brought about by the unpredictability of care available to them in the form of comfort, food, care, and security. Detachment responses can develop where this unpredictability in the infant's care and environment is extreme so that the infant will never be certain that they will be fed, cared for, soothed, or their nappy changed. Critically, it has a negative impact on the infant's sense of self in terms of their own feelings and creates a distorted sense of the environment in which they have to survive.

P

Parentified/caretaker child

Although a parentified (caretaker) child has formed an attachment relationship with their primary carer and internalised good primary experiences with them, they experienced a sense of loss before they were ready to let go of their identification with their carer. This early separation and trauma prevented them from developing a strong sense of self. The experience of the loss of their carer has traumatised them to the extent that it has prevented them from attaching to another carer, becoming instead their own 'caretaker' and taking on a self-parenting role. Although the child or young person is able to think about their unbearable feelings, they are susceptible to emotional outbursts because of a deep sense of sadness and anger. Importantly, they can be reached emotionally by others through communication, because they have the capacity to think about their actions which can prevent the acting out associated with feelings of panic and rage. The worker's task is to encourage the child to hand over the responsibility of the 'little self' to the adult in the confidence that they will take over the responsibilities that the child has carried on their own and to help them to manage transitions in their day-to-day living.

The primary experience

The provision of a **'good' primary experience** (Dockar-Drysdale, 1990) is critical to the emotional development of the infant and subsequently the child and young person. A good primary experience is one where the infant's needs of attunement, being held in mind, love, emotional, and physical security from their primary carer, are met. This is the starting point for emotional integration and the development of their own identity. In contrast, a child or young person who has not experienced the early love and security of a good primary experience, because of neglect, ambivalent parenting, or abuse, is left feeling emotionally abandoned and isolated, and needing to experience that missing primary experience before they can grow emotionally as an individual. Within a therapeutic environment, workers have the knowledge and skills to provide the missing primary experience, allowing opportunities for the child or young person to regress to experiences and behaviours of early childhood. This process enables them to begin the process of emotional integration and the development of their own identity.

Play

Play provides an important range of benefits for children and young people. It is a source of fun and learning. Play develops children's health and relieves stress through physical play; develops insight and understanding of their environment and the people within it through role play and pretend play; develops fine motor skills, language, and musical skills; develops boundaries, social and interactive relationships through shared play and games with rules; and develops creativity, curiosity, and problem-solving through solitary play. Within a therapeutic setting, play is an important element in developing children's emotional, social, and cognitive development. It enables the child or young person to communicate emotions, fears, their sense of self, and the environment in which they live in a symbolic way, where the child or young person is unable to verbalise the depth of their anxiety, fear, or the way they feel about themselves. Observing a child or young person's pretend play can provide the carer or worker with important clues and insight into how the child or young person sees and understands both themselves and the world in which they live. The child can express anger and fear to the extent of annihilating a building they have built, but equally, they can express affection but only towards a particular or favourite toy or doll. They may find it difficult to share, take turns, or accept failure or rivalry and certainly be unable to accept the need for reparation by saying 'sorry' for their behaviour or actions whilst playing with another child. Play, if understood by the carer or worker as an important form of communication, provides an invaluable starting point for insight into the child or young person's world that also offers opportunities for emotional, cognitive, and social growth and language development.

T

Therapeutic environment

Therapeutic environment refers to the characteristics and philosophy of the setting in which children and young people who have experienced profound trauma are cared for, and live. A therapeutic setting is characterised by a holistic psychotherapeutic-informed culture, where the philosophy and values support the care of children and young people who live with profound trauma and, where the carers and workers who live alongside them, share a common psychotherapeutic-informed understanding about how to address their needs, emotions, and behaviours, enabling them to develop and grow. The central task of a therapeutic setting is to enable profoundly traumatised children and young people to develop a stronger and more integrated sense of self and functioning, where they are able to communicate, accept the consequences of their actions, behaviour, and emotions, and grow towards achieving autonomy and independence. At the same time, a therapeutic environment also has a responsibility to support and develop the carers and workers who live alongside these children and young people, addressing issues of vicarious trauma and burnout.

Transitional object

Transitional object normally refers to an object such as a piece of blanket or soft toy that a young infant or child is attached to, and which provides them with comfort and security at times of need, such as when separated from their primary carer. The child can use the transitional object as a bridge or stepping stone to connect their inner world with the outer world. Winnicott viewed attachment to a transitional object as representing an essential phase of ego development leading to the establishment of the young child's sense of self. Importantly, Winnicott (1971: 10) wrote that, 'It is not the object, of course, that is transitional. The object represents the infant's transition from a state of being merged with the mother to a state of being in relation to the mother as something outside and separate'.

Triggers

Triggers occur through either unintended internal or environmental experiences that bring back powerful lived experiences of past trauma, especially where post-traumatic stress disorder exists. These may include personal experiences of fast heartbeat during exercise triggering a fight and flight response experienced during violence or abuse, through to a particular smell or scent, a sound, loud noises in particular contexts such as fireworks, particular places, such as the smell and sounds of being in a hospital, a physical characteristic, or tone of voice associated by a perpetrator, and may result in flashbacks, panic attacks, intense anxiety, sadness, or a sense of being overwhelmed or helpless.

V

Vicarious trauma

Carers and workers who live alongside profoundly traumatised children and young people and who aim to care and work with them in a therapeutic setting are vulnerable to stress and **vicarious trauma**, resulting in burnout, and ultimately, leading to high staff turnover in the profession. The British Medical

Association (BMA) (2020) lists the following cognitive and emotional characteristics as symptoms of vicarious trauma:

- Experiencing lingering feelings of anger, rage, and sadness about patient's victimisation
- Becoming overly involved emotionally with the patient
- Experiencing bystander guilt, shame, and feelings of self-doubt
- Being preoccupied with thoughts of patients outside of the work situation
- Over-identification with the patient (having horror and rescue fantasies)
- Loss of hope, pessimism, and cynicism
- Distancing, numbing, detachment, cutting patients off, and staying busy. Avoiding listening to the client's story of traumatic experiences
- Difficulty in maintaining professional boundaries with the client

Learning to use the Needs Led Assessment model, Therapeutic Treatment Programme, and the carer/worker Reflective Log

Christine Bradley and Francia Kinchington

The Needs Led Assessment model is set out in this chapter using a step-by-step approach illustrated by exemplar material, which focuses on the child/young person's needs, complexity, history, behaviour, and age. It is important to recognise that the Needs Led Assessment and the accompanying Therapeutic Treatment Programme form a package that is totally focused on the needs of the child or young person. The accompanying carer/worker Reflective Log is a critical part of the process as it offers a unique opportunity for the key carer or worker directly involved with the child or young person to reflect on the process of interacting with them, providing a space for their personal feelings and experience to be recorded, in addition to positive progress made by the child/young person or issues arising as they occur.

The relationship between the Needs Led Assessment and Therapeutic Treatment Programme is presented as a **four-stage model** (Figure 3.1) and comprises sets of key questions related to different syndromes of disorganised attachment, including:

- **Frozen**
- **Fragmented/archipelago**
- **Parentified/caretaker**
- **Fragile integration**

These will present the starting point for the team in working therapeutically with the child or young person.

The Needs Led Assessment and Therapeutic Treatment Programmes are designed to understand and address the symptomatic behaviour of an unintegrated child or young person. This process helps to identify the level of privation, deprivation, and trauma which has been experienced in the child's early life and examines how these experiences have influenced and prevented the young person's emotional and cognitive maturation.

The assessment framework followed by a Therapeutic Treatment Programme identifies the quality of support and provision they require if they are to recover from their traumatic and abusive early experiences. This offers the team a starting point and indicative diagnosis which enables them to ascertain whether the child or young person has reached a given point, and critically, the direction they need

DOI: 10.4324/9781032657592-3

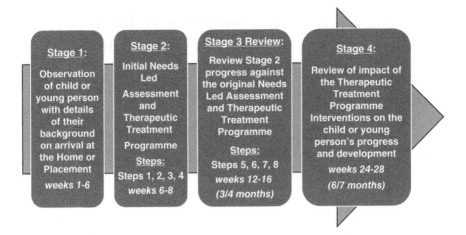

Figure 3.1 Four-stage model showing the relationship between the initial observation of the child or young person and the Need Assessment and Therapeutic Treatment Programmes.

to travel in if they are to recover from their point of breakdown. The scope of the intervention and contingency plans must be thought through so that the young person is supported throughout should a breakdown occur. Carrying out the Needs Led Assessment and Therapeutic Treatment Programme also helps the team to identify the knowledge, understanding, and skills they require to support the child or young person to progress beyond the point of breakdown.

Figure 3.1 shows the four stages that need to be followed over a 28-week period. This commences with an initial observation of a child (Stage 1 during weeks 1–6), through to the initial Needs led Assessment and Therapeutic Treatment Programme for the child, (Stage 2 during weeks 6–8), progressing to the Stage 3 review of progress that takes place during weeks 12–16, and finally the Stage 4 review of the impact of the therapeutic treatment plan and the child's progress that takes place in weeks 24–28.

STAGE 1: OBSERVATION WITH DETAILS OF CHILD/YOUNG PERSON'S BACKGROUND

Stage 1 comprises a period of observation of the child or young person on their arrival at the Residential Home or foster placement.

STAGE 2: DEVELOPING THE NEEDS LED ASSESSMENT AND THERAPEUTIC TREATMENT PROGRAMME (STEPS 1–4)

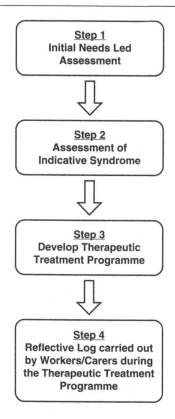

Figure 3.2 Stage 2 (Steps 1–4).

Figure 3.2 sets out Steps 1-4 which describe the steps between carrying out an initial Needs Led Assessment through to developing a Therapeutic Treatment Programme and finalised with the completion of a worker's/carers Reflective Log.

STAGE 3: REVIEW OF PROGRESS AND MODIFICATION OF THERAPEUTIC TREATMENT PROGRAMME (STEPS 5–8)

Stage 3 takes place after a three-month period (Weeks 12–16) and comprises Steps 5–8 and involves carrying out a new initial Needs Led Assessment during which key questions are used to review progress and the initial assessment of the indicative syndrome. This is used to develop an appropriate Therapeutic Treatment Programme in line with changes and development. A carer/worker Reflective Log is kept whilst carrying out the Therapeutic Treatment Programme.

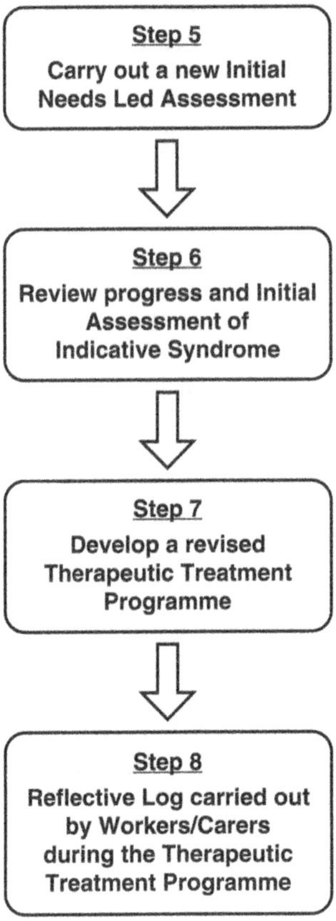

Step 5

Carry out a new Initial
Needs Led Assessment

Step 6

Review progress and Initial
Assessment of
Indicative Syndrome

Step 7

Develop a revised
Therapeutic Treatment
Programme

Step 8

Reflective Log carried out
by Workers/Carers
during the Therapeutic
Treatment Programme

Figure 3.3 Stage 3 (Steps 5–8).

Figure 3.3 describes Steps 5-8, showing how the earlier process (Figure 3.2) is repeated, carrying out a new Needs Led Assessment through to developing a Therapeutic Treatment Plan and finalised with the completion of a worker's/ carers Reflective Log.

**STAGE 4: EVALUATION OF THE IMPACT OF THE THERAPEU-
TIC TREATMENT PROGRAMME INTERVENTION**

The evaluation that takes place after a six-month period (during Weeks 24–28) is critical. It enables the team responsible for the child or young person to review the impact of the Therapeutic Treatment Programme Interventions on the child or young person's progress and development based on the initial observations (Stage 1), the two Needs Led Assessments, the focus of the Therapeutic Treatment Programmes, and the insight offered by the carer/key worker's Reflective Log (Stages 2 and 3). This allows for professional discussions about the young person's progress and development to take place based on the evidence gathered over this period of time and to plan for future actions and further potential intervention.

GUIDANCE NOTES: CARRYING OUT THE INITIAL NEEDS LED ASSESSMENT

The following guidance is advised in carrying out the Stage 2 Needs Led Assessment which follows the Observation period.

- The assessment meeting should involve all carers and workers who are or have been engaged in the child's life over the six weeks following the child or young person's placement following the initial Stage 1 Observation.
- The chair of the meeting and everyone involved should have as much information as possible about the first few years of the child's life, their relationship with their primary carer, and any significant events.
- The Needs Led Assessment should only be carried out when the child or young person has been in their placement for six to eight weeks to ensure that as much information has been gathered about the child or young person in terms of their background and them in situ in the placement.
- Not all the questions on the assessment form (Table 3.1) need to be asked. Identify and focus on the most appropriate three or four questions that will help the team to gain a deeper understanding of the needs of the child. This discussion will last approximately two hours.
- The meeting often views the child as fitting into different aspects of the syndromes of deprivation. It is normal that there should be a variety of thoughts and ideas from professionals in the meeting. The syndrome which brings out the strongest agreement in the meeting about the child should be the one to be used as the focus for the Therapeutic Treatment Programme.

Step 1: key questions that help identify an indicative assessment

The team of workers is asked to consider and respond to the questions listed below in relation to the individual child or young person who is the focus of the Needs Led Assessment. There are seven categories which need to be considered, accompanied by sets of key questions which are central to the Needs Led Assessment. The categories comprise in general: boundaries, merging and functioning; containing emotion, anxiety, anger, and stress; self-destruction and self-preservation; communication; learning from experience and play. Although an affirmative response to the questions relates to an indicative characteristic of one of the three potential assessments of frozen, fragmented/archipelago, or parentified/caretaker as classifications of fragmented/disorganised attachment, it is also important to recognise that the responses to some questions may relate to all three assessments and so should be considered in the context of the overall indicative assessment so that responses and the Therapeutic Treatment Programme can be tailored to the needs of the child or young person.

Table 3.1 Step 1: Identifying the relationship between categories, questions, and indicative assessment

Category	Question	i Answer Yes or No. ii If Yes – give an example or explanation for this decision	If Yes– initial indicative assessment
1. Self-esteem	1. Are there concerns about the child's sense of self and their self-esteem?		**This is applicable to all categories but with varying responses and needs to be thought about in the context of responses to the other categories and questions.**
2. Boundaries, merging and functioning	1. Does the child merge and disrupt the functioning of others?		**Frozen**
	2. Does the child have any areas of functioning?		**Fragmented/ archipelago**
	3. Is help needed when functioning breaks down or can the child manage stress and transitions?		**Fragmented/ archipelago**
	4. When under extreme stress, does the child merge and disrupt the functioning of others?		**Parentified/ caretaker**

(Continued)

Table 3.1 (Continued)

Category	Question	i Answer Yes or No. ii If Yes – give an example or explanation for this decision	If Yes– initial indicative assessment
3. Containing emotion, anxiety, anger, and stress	1. Can the child contain emotions, or do they act out violently?		**Frozen**
	2. Does the child act out violently when under stress?		**Fragmented/ archipelago**
	3. Do they react violently under pressure or perceived threat?		**Parentified/ caretaker**
4. Self-destruction and self-preservation	1. Does the child have very low self-esteem and is unable to take care of themselves?		**Frozen**
	2. When under stress, does the child engage in a range of self-destruction behaviours, e.g., self-mutilation or suicidal gestures?		**Fragmented/ archipelago**
	3. Can they protect themselves? Is their self-preservation haphazard?		**Parentified/ caretaker**
5. Communication (symbolic, verbal, and non-verbal)	1. Can the child talk meaningfully in a one-to-one situation, or do they just chatter without meaning?		**Frozen**

(Continued)

Table 3.1 (Continued)

Category	Question	i Answer Yes or No. ii If Yes – give an example or explanation for this decision	If Yes– initial indicative assessment
	2. Is there the potential for some communication, but they back off when anxious or stressed?		**Fragmented/ archipelago**
	3. Does the child communicate in a way that is not easily understood and often symbolic?		**Caretaker**
6. Capacity to recover by learning from experience	1. Does the child find it difficult to learn from their personal, social, and school experiences, including mistakes?		**Frozen**
	2. Does the child have the potential to learn cognitively and emotionally through communication but is unable to it when under stress?		**Fragmented/ archipelago**
	3. Does the child find learning at school a difficult experience?		**Parentified/ caretaker**

(Continued)

Table 3.1 (Continued)

Category	Question	i Answer Yes or No. ii If Yes – give an example or explanation for this decision	If Yes– initial indicative assessment
	4. Does the child have difficulty in learning from setbacks and picking up and continuing where they left from?		**This is applicable to all categories but with varying responses and needs to be thought about in the context of responses to the other categories and questions.**
	5. Does the child have any strategies to show that they are able to learn from experience?		**This is applicable to all categories but with varying responses and needs to be thought about in the context of responses to the other categories and questions.**
7. Capacity to accept personal responsibility for their actions	1. Does the child find it difficult to anticipate consequences?		**This is applicable to all categories but with varying responses and needs to be thought about in the context of responses to the other categories and questions.**

(Continued)

Table 3.1 (Continued)

Category	Question	i Answer Yes or No. ii If Yes – give an example or explanation for this decision	If Yes– initial indicative assessment
	2. Does the child find it difficult to anticipate or think about their future?		**This is applicable to all categories but with varying responses and needs to be thought about in the context of responses to the other categories and questions.** **Essentially, has the child created their own reality so their future is of their own making, rather than them being located in the real world.**
8. Play	1. Is the child's play easily distracted and sometimes destructive?		**Fragmented/ archipelago**
	2. Can the child play, but at an infantile level?		**Parentified/ caretaker**
9. Fragile integration	1. Can the child hold onto boundaries, but push them in an anti-authority way, especially under stress?		**Indicative assessment: fragile integration**
	2. Do they disintegrate when very anxious and are unable to talk about stress?		

(Continued)

Table 3.1 (Continued)

Category	Question	i Answer Yes or No. ii If Yes – give an example or explanation for this decision	If Yes– initial indicative assessment
	3. Under stress do they lack self-esteem and self-care, can they become self-destructive? 4. Is communication predominantly at a symbolic level with little investment in verbal communication? 5. Does the child find it difficult to face reality and, when unable to communicate their anxiety, act out through anti-social behaviour? 6. Does the child have a general commitment to school and the experiences which are offered to them? 7. Does the child engage in solitary or cooperative play?		

Step 2: interpreting the potential initial indicative assessment

1 Total the number of responses from the right-hand column of Table 3.1 according to each of the following four categories: fragmented/archipelago, frozen, parentified/caretaker, and fragile integration.
2 Now summarise these responses in Table 3.2.

Table 3.2 Summary of responses to identify indicative assessment

Fragmented/ archipelago	Frozen	Parentified/ caretaker	Fragile integration: Yes/No

It is likely that a range of indicative assessments will be identified; however, the highest number of responses within a single assessment category will give you an indication of the most relevant assessment of the child or young person. This will then inform the basis of the Therapeutic Treatment Programme.

Step 3: developing an appropriate Therapeutic Treatment Programme

i Prioritise three areas from the list below which the team feels need to be worked through as a matter of priority with the child or young person. These will form the focus of the child or young person's Therapeutic Treatment Programme set out in Table 3.3.

Table 3.3 Identifying priorities to create an appropriate Therapeutic Treatment Programme

	Therapeutic Treatment Programme category	Indicate priority
1	Self-esteem	
2	Boundaries, merging and functioning	
3	Containing emotion, anxiety, anger, and stress	
4	Self-destruction and self-preservation	
5	Communication (symbolic, verbal, and non-verbal)	
6	Capacity to recover by learning from experience	
7	Capacity to accept personal responsibility for their actions	
8	Play	
9	Fragile integration	

Table 3.4 Creating the Therapeutic Treatment Programme

Category	Therapeutic Treatment Programme

ii Transfer the three priority areas from Table 3.3 onto Table 3.4 (to create the Therapeutic Treatment Programme). Read through the responses and exemplars that you have listed initially in Table 3.1, and use Chapter 2: 'Understanding the vocabulary of working with children and young people who have experienced profound trauma', to help the team to interpret the assessment and to create an appropriate Treatment Programme based on the priorities identified for the child or young person. It is important to decide what will take place on a daily basis on the child/young person's return from school, for example, offering the child/young person a hot drink and biscuit and talking about how their day has been); providing specialist activities that will take place once or twice a week (e.g. play therapy); action which takes place on a 'need' basis (e.g. when the child loses control).

GUIDANCE NOTES: CREATING THE THERAPEUTIC TREATMENT PROGRAMME

A follow-up Needs Led Assessment meeting on the individual child or young person should take place after a three-month period (during Weeks 12–16). The three-step process is repeated as for Stage 2 and focused on building on the progress made during Stage 2. It is important to take the carer/key worker's reflective log into account and the insight this provides into the adult-child relationship, the degree of anxiety held by the key adult in interacting with the child/young person, and whether there are any indications of carer/worker vulnerability, transference and countertransference in their engagement, or other areas which need to be addressed.

The refocused 24-hour Treatment (or identified period) Programme is aimed at supporting the continued development of the child or young person within a set time period.

The following examples of practice show what carers and workers need to understand and how they can develop appropriate Therapeutic Treatment Programmes in relation to the key areas listed as follows:

Being held in mind

- A child needs to feel that the carer or worker on whom they are becoming dependent continues to think about them even when not with the child physically. For example, if the carer or worker suddenly has to be away for a period of time, it is important that they can help the child to believe that they continue to think about them. They can do this by writing a note for the child to receive each day they are not with them in Home. This will enable the child to feel that their carer or worker is holding them in their mind. This is important as it helps the child to begin the process of becoming emotionally secure enough to become more able to start developing a significant attachment relationship with their carer or key worker.
- Help the child or young person to believe that you are thinking about their individual needs. For example, each day when they return from school spend some time with them individually to talk about their school day and how it went for them. Provide them with a drink in a special mug which belongs to them individually. This will help them to bring together both their positive and negative feelings about functioning in school.
- Help them to believe that they matter as individuals in their own right. This could help them to make significant attachment relationships with those who are responsible for them, feeling that they can be taken seriously, listened to, and heard with meaning and sincerity from their carer or key worker. This one-to-one interaction that is focused on the child is central to the therapeutic process and one which contributes to developing a positive sense of self.

Providing a primary experience

- It is important to remember that a child who has been exposed to early experiences of trauma, hostility, and ongoing conflict with parental figures in their life did not have the security of a primary experience with their primary carer and as a consequence, is left with little or no feeling of self-worth. It makes it very difficult for them to manage the challenges of the outside world, because they did not receive any early positive experiences for themselves. This makes it very difficult for them. The majority of these traumatised children and young people did not have the opportunity to play as a young child through which they were able to express their anxiety or emotions, and as a result, they felt left with overwhelming unbearable emotions that they were unable to manage.
- A good primary experience represents a latency or adolescent young person being able to 'play out' some of their earlier feelings. This can be created either through play or using elements of creativity.
- The lost child in them needs to experience being recognised as the child who did lose out on them being able to think about their feelings and

manage them positively. For example, a ten-year-old boy who had felt emotionally abandoned as a small child because he had to look after his four younger siblings when their mother left them, was able to work through some of his ambivalence about his early years by having a toy kitchen where he played at cooking for everybody until he no longer needed to. The workers allowed him to work through the trauma of his early childhood experiences, so that he began to believe that he could let go of his anger and sadness which had been left inside him. He then started to function like a 10–11-year-old rather than a small child who felt on his own and emotionally abandoned.

- Workers need to believe that it is never too late to provide a traumatised child with a good primary experience where they feel looked after and which they missed out on as a small child.

Managing transitions

- The task here is to help the child or young person to be able to manage changes in their life whether it be emotional or in reality. The child needs to have internalised enough good and positive early experiences in their life which they can hold onto. This is particularly important when a child is faced with multiple foster or residential placements. This involves separation from their placement and moving to another placement, with new people and possibly in a different part of the country, and a new school.

- It is important that carers and workers understand the differences between the child's internal reality and meeting the challenges of the external world. Managing transitions becomes complex and a major source of anxiety where children and young people have an experience of powerlessness and being traumatised through previous traumatic and negative transitions that they have previously experienced.

- It is important that carers and worker understand the role of, and use of, transitional objects that are discussed in the needs assessment profiles.

- Being able to help the child or young person to make a good transition from one stage of their life to another requires that they have taken in and internalised the memory of a good experience which they can live with and use, providing a foundation for them to emotionally develop into the next stage of their life. It is important that carers and workers recognise that for some of the children and young people they are responsible for, the experience of transition may bring up both positive and negative behaviours and they may 'act out' whilst they are managing the transition. It all depends on previous experiences they have encountered in their lives. Help them to work through their unbearable feelings and offer opportunities for these to be communicated whether symbolically, non-verbally, or verbally.

Symbolic communication

- It is important to recognise that not all children and young people are able to find the words to communicate their fears and anxieties in their day-to-day living, since the pain and anger of the trauma that they have experienced is literally unspeakable.
- We have to realise that these children and young people will 'speak' to us in their own ways.
- It is crucial in therapeutic treatment that carers and workers are able to understand the way that the pain and anxiety are being expressed by the child/young person and to respond rather than react to their behaviour when they cannot verbally communicate their distress and feelings. Their inability to express their anger, their anxiety, and how they feel about themselves results in the likelihood that the child/young person will 'act out' destructively towards others, or self-destructively towards themselves.
- If the child's level of functioning diminishes, the carer or worker should take the initiative and raise the subject by asking the child/young person whether there is anything they are experiencing which is making them particularly anxious and whether there is anything that the carer or worker can do to help them.
- It is important that workers understand what is meant by symbolic and non-verbal communication. The child or young person can often express themselves in other ways. This can be through helping the child/young person to find creative outlets through which they can express themselves, such as through art, play, or music. It is important that carers and workers can respond effectively to the communication and the way that it is expressed, and understand that it can take the form of creative or destructive functioning. Whether positive or negative, the expression provides a starting point for communication.

Relating to the outside world without merging

- A traumatised child who is overwhelmed with feelings and anxieties they cannot think about may have little or no sense of self. This can mean that they are constantly looking for another person whose identity is as fragile as theirs to form a bond with.
- A merger is the joining together of two or more young people in anti-social and destructive activity. It can be extremely hard for the carers or workers to interrupt and calm them down when their fury with the outside world overwhelms them.
- The experience is complex, since the child or young person has over-identified, and is engulfed by their own unbearable feelings of rage and despair. They have never had the experience of being aware of an adult

holding them in their mind, and feeling emotionally contained by them, and because they have never felt emotionally contained by an adult, they experience the outside 'real' world as being hostile and being there to attack them, in fact mirroring their own inner world and experiences. Their response then is that the outside world is one which needs to be attacked.

- To help the child or young person to move forward as their own sense of self starts to develop, they need to feel, and 'believe', that there is a person (their carer or key worker) who is preoccupied with them as an individual, and who can respond to them accordingly. This will vary according to the level of emotional development that the child/young person has reached. A child who is beginning to develop a sense of self, but remains deeply vulnerable and fragile at times, requires considerable emotional support from the workers. In contrast, a child or young person who remains in a very unintegrated stage of development with little, or no sense of self, needs to believe that those responsible for them can adapt to their needs through responding to their extreme and intense emotions of panic and rage which they cannot as yet start to think about. It is important that the differences that exist in the stage of emotional development between these two categories are understood and responded to appropriately by the workers if they are either to strengthen or help child/young person to begin to develop a sense of self which they can feel more comfortable with. Having a stronger sense of self will help prevent them from seeking to merge with others and to share their anti-social behaviour. The risk of merging with another lessens as the child/young person starts to believe that they are a person in their own right, one who can find a place for themselves in the outside world where they feel that they belong and can become a part of the group setting.

Transference and countertransference

- Transference and countertransference are crucial concepts that should be understood by all who work therapeutically with traumatised children and young people.
- Transference is the process where a child or young person transfers feelings and ideas which derive from their earlier experiences of hostility and abuse from previous parental figures in their past, onto those taking care of them. The result can be that they respond to their current carer as though they were the original attacking parental figure, anticipating that they will be as physically and verbally abused by them as happened in their earlier years. This can result in life feeling quite unbearable for them and can result in them acting out their panic and rage, which, unless understood by their worker, can result in dire consequences causing negative outcomes for them.

- Countertransference describes the response of carers/workers working closely with seriously traumatised children and young people in a variety of settings who find themselves responding emotionally to the young person's complex, primitive behaviour, and anxiety. If the care/worker has poor interpersonal boundaries and becomes receptive to the child's or young person's overwhelming emotions, they may find it very difficult to contain their own emotions in response to the child and their behaviour. They may feel anger, anxiety, frustration, and even a sense of powerlessness when they interact with the child, and critically, feel unable to help or support them.
- Left unresolved, transference and countertransference between carers/ workers and the child or young person can be re-enacted, becoming an ongoing saga which can result in negative outcomes for the child/young person and the adults who care for them.
- It is essential that workers and carers are able to reflect on their own responses, emotions, and reactions to the children and young people for whom they are responsible so that they are able to identify whether their emotional responses arise as a consequence of the young person transferring onto them, or whether, critically, the child's behaviour and emotional responses reawaken repressed experiences and emotions in the carer/ worker themselves, and so questions the adult's relationship with the child or young person.
- Unresolved early feelings affect the child's thought patterns in later relationships, particularly if they are overwhelmed with unbearable anxiety and fear which they have never been able to express, and ultimately affect their capacity to manage the challenges of later life. If the child or young person transfers their fears and anxieties onto their carer and it is not responded to appropriately, they can react destructively towards themselves or others.
- Reflective practice is crucial for carers and workers if they are to develop their own insight and understanding about the complexity of providing therapeutic treatment and practise, with those they are responsible for and identifying and developing a working practise which meets their primary needs helping the child or young person to develop a stronger sense of self. This is not an easy task for carers/workers, and at the end of each day, the team collectively should have the opportunity to discuss how they feel about working with those for whom they are responsible. Understanding the emotional life of the young person, their fragility, and identifying what it is they can anticipate from the young person the following day, and importantly, the strategies they can use in response to the young person's behaviour. This will enable the carer/worker to separate their own emotional response to the child and respond calmly and appropriately to the young person's behaviour, preventing their behaviour from escalating. Importantly, this offers an alternative scenario to the child/young person, countering the re-enactment that they are currently locked into.

GUIDANCE NOTES: NEEDS LED ASSESSMENT PROFORMA

The Needs Led Assessment Proforma (Table 3.5) is used to record the outcome of the Needs Led Assessment that is carried out on a child/ young person with the key worker and team directly responsible for them. Exemplars for Needs Led Assessment and 24-hour care/given period Therapeutic Treatment Programmes are provided in Chapter 4 of the handbook.

Table 3.5 Needs Led Assessment Proforma

Needs Led Assessment Proforma

Identifying and understanding the trauma experienced by the child or adolescence is the first step in creating a meaningful Needs Led Assessment and Treatment Programme. This understanding helps the team to understand the symptoms of behaviour in an unintegrated child or adolescent whose maturation and developmental processes have been disrupted because of early life experiences of trauma abandonment, abuse, and deprivation.

The outcome of the assessment is to create a treatment programme which identifies the support, communication, and provision the child or young person requires to help them to begin a process of recovery.

<u>Needs Led Assessment and Therapeutic Treatment Programme</u>   Name: of child/
<u>Programme</u>   young person
<u>Dob:</u>
<u>Name of Centre:</u>

Name of Child:
Team Present:
1
2
3
4
5
Centre:
Date:

Is this the first Needs Led Assessment? Yes/No
If No give date/s of earlier Needs Led Assessments:

Treatment Programme category		Indicate as appropriate
1	Self-esteem	
2	Boundaries, merging and functioning	
3	Containing emotion, anxiety, anger, and stress	
4	Self-destruction and self-preservation	
5	Communication (symbolic, verbal, and non-verbal)	
6	Capacity to recover by learning from experience	
7	Capacity to accept personal responsibility for their actions	
8	Play	
9	Fragile integration	

Focus of Therapeutic Treatment Programme

1 <u>Self-esteem</u>
2 <u>Boundaries, merging and functioning</u>
3 <u>Containing emotion, anxiety, anger, and stress</u>
4 <u>Self-destruction and self-preservation</u>
5 <u>Communication (symbolic, verbal, non-verbal)</u>
6 <u>Capacity to recover by learning from experience</u>
7 <u>Capacity to accept personal responsibility for their actions</u>
8 <u>Play</u>
9 <u>Fragile integration</u>

Step 3: Therapeutic Treatment Programme (based on the priority areas identified set within a 24-hour, or identified period timeframe)

<u>Conclusion</u>

Follow-up Needs Led Assessment: date for next meeting

Date:

STEP 4: GUIDANCE NOTES
CARER/KEY WORKER REFLECTIVE LOG

Table 3.6 presents a model for a carer/worker Reflective Log. Completing this enables the carer or worker interacting directly with the child or young person to record their experiences, personal insight, emotional response, and to reflect on how the interaction impacts on them emotionally and professionally.

Table 3.6 Carer/key worker Reflective Log

CARER/KEY WORKER REFLECTIVE LOG   Name of child/young person
The aim of this log is to enable you to record a short reflective account following your interaction with a child or young person with whom you are working. This will help create a record that will enable you to monitor progress over time. Although you do not need to use these headings, you may find them useful as a starting point.

Name of the child/young person	date	time spent with the child/ young person
Summary of what took place and outcome in terms of progress (whether forward or retrograde)		
The child/young person's capacity to manage their internal world and external reality		

Observations re child/young person's use of symbolic, verbal, and non-verbal communication

Observation of the child/young person's emotional experience of the interaction

How did you feel in anticipation, prior to the interaction with the child/young person?

How did you feel afterwards, once the interaction was over?

On reflection, what advice would you give yourself?

Issues that need to be discussed at next meeting with line manager: • In relation to the child/young person • Self in relation to capacity to manage the young person's behaviour • Need for additional training

Chapter 4

Exemplars that address the legacy of early trauma

Christine Bradley

This chapter presents case studies drawn from practice that reflect the key categories of frozen, fragmented/archipelago, parentified/caretaker child, and fragile ego-integration. The selection of and reasoning behind the areas for development are presented within the case studies based on the child/young person's need. In addition to the initial Needs Led Assessment (NLA), the case studies include the team's use of the Therapeutic Treatment Programme (TTP) and in the new three-stage model, the workers/carers' reflective log (Table 4.1).

The case studies are presented in two forms:

i **A new three-stage model is presented which comprises:**

- Stage 1: a NLA, a guided TTP, and if appropriate, key areas of training and development needed by the carer/team that would enable them to work more effectively with the child/young person.
- Stage 2: a reflective log to be written by the team working directly with the child/young person to explore their own experience of interacting with the young person, their emotions, and identifying any emergent issues and training needs.
- Stage 3: a new NLA and guided TTP is carried out three months after the initial NLA and guided Therapeutic Treatment Plan. The aim of this is for the team to review the child/young person's progress and identify new areas of their development that will enable the carer or team to focus on whilst working with the child/young person.

ii **The original model comprising NLA and TTP**

DOI: 10.4324/9781032657592-4

Table 4.1 Case studies which include a carer/workers' Reflective Log in addition to the Needs Led Assessment (NLA) and Therapeutic Treatment Programme (TTP)

New three-stage model	Assessment	Areas for development
Tom **age 10**	Fragmented/ archipelago	First NLA and TTP: • Boundaries, merging and functioning • Containing emotion, anxiety, anger, and stress
		Second NLA and TTP: • Boundaries, merging and functioning • Containing emotion, anxiety, anger, and stress • Communication (symbolic, verbal, and non-verbal)
Charlie **age 9**	Approaching fragile integration	First NLA and TTP: • Containing emotion, anxiety, anger, and stress • Self-esteem and self-preservation
		Second NLA and TTP: • Containing emotion, anxiety, anger, and stress • Communication
George **age 12**	Fragile integrated	First NLA and TTP: • Containing emotions, anxiety, anger, and stress • Communication
		Second NLA and TTP: • Containing emotion, anxiety, anger, and stress • Learning from experience

(Continued)

Table 4.1 (Continued)

Original model	Assessment	Areas for development
Amy age 11 NLA 1 TTP	Frozen	• Boundaries, merging and functioning • Containing emotion, anxiety, anger, and stress
Jimmy age 12 NLA 1 TTP	Fragmented/ archipelago	• Containing emotion, anxiety, anger, and stress • Self-esteem and self-preservation • Separation and loss, managing transitions
Jessica age 15 NLA 1 TTP	Parentified/caretaker	• Containing emotion, anxiety, anger, and stress • Self-esteem and self-preservation • Communication
Kiera age 14 NLA 1 TTP	Fragmented/ archipelago with a frozen sense of self	• Boundaries, merging and functioning • Containing emotion, anxiety, anger, and stress

CASE STUDIES USING THE NEW THREE-PART MODEL

Case Study 1: Tom *(Fragmented/Archipelago)*

NLA Proforma

Identifying and understanding the trauma experienced by the child or adolescence is the first step in creating a meaningful Needs Led Assessment and Treatment Programme. This understanding helps the team to understand the symptoms of behaviour in an unintegrated child or adolescent whose maturation and developmental processes have been disrupted because of early life experiences of trauma abandonment, abuse, and deprivation.

The outcome of the assessment is to create a treatment programme which identifies the support, communication, and provision the child or young person requires to help them to begin a process of recovery.

Needs Led Assessment and Therapeutic Treatment   Name: TOM
Programme
Name of Centre:

Name of Child: Tom	Date:

Team Present:

1 Manager
2 Shift leader
3 Residential worker
4 Senior residential worker
5 Residential care worker
6 Deputy manager
7 Play therapist
8 Psychotherapist
9 Christine Bradley Consultant Psychotherapist

Date of meeting:

Has a previous Needs Led Assessment and Therapeutic Treatment Programme taken place? **No**

If Yes: give date

Step 1: background

Tom spent the first four years of his early life living with his family who were travellers. It was reported to be a very dysfunctional family where it was thought that Tom experienced considerable episodes of domestic and possibly sexual abuse. In 2018 at the age of four years of age, the social services responsible for him, decided that the family home was not a safe place for him in which to live. It was viewed as an emotionally fragmented home where he lacked any positive emotional stimulation which contributed to his considerable learning difficulties.

Initially, he was placed for one night with a couple in their home, but his uncontained behaviour meant they could not hold onto him and he was transferred to a single foster parent where he stayed for a several years and where he felt emotionally contained and nurtured. However, the arrival of COVID led to his placement having to end as he was at a high risk of catching it. This was followed by Tom being placed into a residential home which was not able to meet his needs or respond to him appropriately, and as a result, he acted out his emotions negatively by exposing himself to other children.

Consequently, the placement broke down and he was placed in the Residential Home in September 2022.

Tom presents himself as being emotionally fragile. He finds it difficult to engage with adults in a meaningful way for any length of time because of his own early traumatic experiences. He expects anything which feels positive for him to break down within a short period, so he creates a situation where it does, and this in turn creates a sense of predictability and security for him. He carries with him fears and uncertainties about positive experiences continuing. To help workers address his need for appropriate therapeutic responses from them, it was agreed that a Needs Led Assessment and a Therapeutic Treatment Plan be carried out.

Step 2: identifying the focus of the Treatment Programme

As part of the discussion, the team are required to assess the level of integration and ego functioning, together with levels of non-functioning of the child, and prioritise between two to four areas which felt are vital to Tom's development and will form the basis of the Treatment Plan.

Of the eight key areas for development, it was agreed to prioritise the following two areas:

1 **Boundaries, merging and functioning**
2 **Containing emotion, anxiety, anger, and stress**

Treatment Programme: key areas for development	Indicate as appropriate
Self-esteem and self-preservation	
Boundaries, merging and functioning	X
Containing emotion, anxiety, anger, and stress	X
Capacity to recover by learning from experience	
Capacity to accept personal responsibility for their actions	
Communication (symbolic, non-verbal, and verbal)	
Play	
Fragile integration	

Focus of Treatment Programme

Boundaries, merging and functioning: observation

Tom often places himself into a 'zone' of emotional isolation, striving to replicate his early experiences of being on his own for a number of periods during his early life, and continues to re-create feelings of emotional isolation for himself. To survive his overwhelming anxieties and uncertainties, he has created a 'false self'. Through the use of the 'false self' (Winnicott, 1953), he can present himself as functioning well; however, the slightest anxiety can result in him breaking down again acting out self-destructively and aggressively, towards others.

Tom has certain parts of his personality which have become frozen and because he has never been able to express his emotions through words, they remain locked inside him. At times, his emotions are uncontrollable and explode from him and he becomes destructive towards others or self-destructive. This means that he finds it difficult, and at times, quite unbearable, to learn from his experiences and accept personal responsibility for his behaviour. Although he can function on a day-to-day basis, at times, anything that he finds stressful can result in him breaking down.

In terms of boundaries, merging and functioning, Tom functions at the level of a fragmented/archipelago child with parts of his emotions remaining frozen. This is because there are so many overwhelming emotions trapped inside his inner world that it is difficult for him to manage the reality of his day-to-day living without considerable and appropriate support from those responsible for him.

Containing emotion, anxiety, anger, and stress: observation

Tom carries many anxieties and uncertainties in his own inner world and he carries the needs of a small child who expects either 100% preoccupation from his workers or he feels left with nothing at all. There is an inner emptiness in Tom where he has not felt 'held in the mind' of adults who are taking care of him. His relationship with his mother was ambivalent because it was either incomplete or not there. As a consequence, his feelings are cut off from his thinking. There is a part of Tom which can function but he requires a great deal of adult support and provision if he is to continue functioning and manage his anxieties and uncertainties.

In this category, Tom is functioning at the level of a fragmented/archipelago child who has become emotionally fragmented in order to survive. This term represents a child who is trapped in the fragmented world of emotions that evolved during their maturational development. This fragmentation occurred because although, at times, Tom experienced a sense of good enough care from his mother, it was inconsistent, lasting only for a short period. Tom's areas of non-functioning are locked into his early infantile state of loss which needs providing for, and adapted to, by his carers if therapeutic practise and treatment is to be successful.

Step 3: Therapeutic Treatment Programme

1 Tom needs to feel and believe that he is being 'held in the mind' of those taking care of him.
2 Remember that his non-functioning periods represent the time when he felt locked into an early infantile state when the appropriate primary provision did not occur, and where as a consequence, he felt emotionally abandoned and isolated.
3 Try to provide Tom with something which is adapted to meet his infantile needs and which represents the fact that you are holding him in your mind.

Topics the team need to think about and identify whether additional training is required on the following:

• What is understood by the 'provision of primary experiences' for fragmented children and young people
• Transference and countertransference in a therapeutic setting

Tom's sense of self is very low and fragile. The reason for the team to examine transference and countertransference is that caring for Tom could bring up some very strong emotions in the workers. There is a very lost child in Tom who needs taking good care of. It is crucial that his carers are able to understand their **own** emotions about working with him and ensure that they are able to hold onto their own boundaries during their contact with him.

It is recognised that a good outcome for Tom would be that over the following months, his fragile sense of self begins to strengthen and come together as his sense of isolation diminishes, and also, that he is able to maintain and develop a more reliable attachment relationship with a worker on whom he is dependent and who can provide for meeting his primary and secondary needs.

Conclusion

A follow-up Needs Led Assessment on Tom needs to be written and discussed in three months' time when his level of emotional integration, personal development, and level of functioning and sense of self can be reviewed.

Follow-up Needs Led Assessment: date to be confirmed

Christine Bradley
Psychotherapist

Date:

Carer/Worker's Reflective Log   **Name: Tom**

The aim of this log is to enable the team to record a short reflective account following each interaction with a child or young person with whom they are working. This will help create a record that will enable them to monitor progress over time.

(Although you do not need to use these headings, you may find them useful as a starting point.)

Name of the child/young person: Tom   **Date:**

Summary of what took place and outcome in terms of progress (whether forward or retrograde)

Examples of progress cited by workers demonstrating insight and understanding about the team's work with Tom:

1   Tom is now more able to take part in a meal with the group in restaurants. Comfortably being a part of the group. *Progress made*
2   Wanted to think about making apple strudel pie with a team member. *Progress*
3   When a member of staff was leaving the Home and came of say goodbye, Tom was able to express his feelings of sadness about her leaving. Thinking and feelings coming together. This shows a sign of hope for Tom's recovery from his traumas. *Progress forward gained*
4   Was able to settle when a book was being read to him at bedtime and listen to the workers reading. More positive that earlier reading experiences from others. *Progress gained*

Retrograde but progress made when worker reached out to him:

5   Left his room after settling down and refused to return to bed, became unregulated and reacted by throwing things around his room, because he was struggling with his inner world of thoughts and feelings; he began to spit, hit out, and act out aggressively. He needed help to understand what was going on in his head. *Retrograde step*

The child/young person's capacity to manage their internal world and external reality

Examples of progress cited by workers:

No change:

1   Tom continues to express feelings of high anxiety when under stressful situations in his day-to-day living. *No change*

Progress made:

2   Tom is now more able to manage activities which have not been planned and simply happen. *Progress gained*
3   Is now more able to manage his internal world becoming aware of his painful feelings and then sharing them with his workers. *Progress gained*
4   Although Tom needs to feel that he is being listened by his workers, he can also communicate his feelings by scribbling them on paper for others to read. *Progress forward*
5   Tom does now have the capacity to understand the pain of external reality but finds it difficult to accept it. He struggles with his internal world at bedtime when he is faced with internal emotions that he finds unbearable to live with. He is not as aggressive as he used to be and wants to understand more about his emotions. *Progress gained*

Observations of child/young person's use of symbolic, verbal, and non-verbal communication

Examples of progress cited by workers:

No change:

1   When Tom becomes anxious and cannot communicate about how he feels. He becomes bouncy and fidgets a great deal. *No change*
2   When under stress, Tom keeps himself busy and becomes non-verbal. Although he does need to know that the worker is listening to him and in touch with how he is feeling. *No change*

Progress made:

3 He is often contented, often in the car when he is being driven, and can start to play symbolically telling stories about himself. *Progress gained*
4 Can verbalise well and show a slight maturity with certain staff members. Also showed signs of symbolic maturity when a staff member he related to left the home. He played with the doll's house which she left for the home as a way of communicating with her though play. *Progress gained*

Retrograde:

5 When Tom becomes non-verbal, he can be aggressive, his facial expressions become anxious, and he can cry and stamp his feet. When verbal he shouts and swears. *Retrospective progress*

Observation of the child/young person's emotional experience of the interaction

Examples of progress cited by workers:

Progress made:

1 Tom needs a safe physical touch from his workers to help calm him down at times.
2 He can become excited when he is happy. We need to be in touch with him at these times and be happy with him.
3 Tom expressed a period of difficult behaviour when a member of staff was leaving, but with help from his worker, he was able to express his feelings of sadness and accepted the help from them to manage his emotions. *Progress gained*
4 There are times when Tom appears quite content after interacting with a worker. *Progress gained*
5 At times, Tom can show frustration, boredom, and a desire to become more independent and make his own rules, whilst at the same time demanding constant positive attention.

How did you feel in anticipation, prior to the interaction with the child/young person?

Workers identified a common theme of anxiety whilst working with Tom:

1 Felt anxious, hope that he will feel stimulated by my interaction with him.
2 Slightly apprehensive and unsure how he was going to manage, and that I would be able to manage his emotions and potential behaviour.

3 Anxious that Tom would try to end our time together before we had reached a deeper understanding about his emotions.

4 Anxious in the hope that he would settle easily once he was in bed, as he had been leaving his room after settling.

How did you feel afterwards, once the interaction was over?

Workers reflected that they made appropriate judgements in relation to Tom, and importantly, that they were in touch with their own feelings following their interactions with him.

1 Calm, safe in my thinking that I had been correct about him for the first time.

2 Fine and content about our interaction together.

3 I felt quiet about how Tom has managed himself and showed that he had progressed during his stay with us.

4 I felt proud and satisfied that Tom had been able to listen to what I was trying to say to him.

5 Tired, after supporting other adults with the altercation. Sad for him as it was not nice seeing him so distraught and unsettled.

On reflection, what advice would you give yourself?

Issues that need to be discussed at the next meeting with the line manager:

- **In relation to the child/young person**
- **Self in relation to the capacity to manage the young person's behaviour**

Observation

We can see through the initial Needs Led Assessment and reflective log that the team have written about their ability to deepen their insight and understanding about meeting Tom's emotional needs which has now become understood and met by them. The following Needs Led Assessment and treatment programme will inform us whether the team's Therapeutic Treatment Programme with Tom has helped him to become more emotionally integrated and more able to understand and communicate about how he is feeling during his day-to-day contact with them.

| Second NLA Proforma + Therapeutic Treatment Programme | Name: TOM |

Needs Led Assessment and Treatment Programme
Name of Centre:

| Name of Child: Tom | Date: |

This is the second Needs Led Assessment and Therapeutic Treatment Plan on Tom and is a review of the progress following the first Needs Led Assessment and Therapeutic Treatment Programme that took place three months ago, and which was aimed to help workers meet the emotional needs of Tom and provide him with the appropriate therapeutic provision.

The outcome of the previous assessment was that Tom's current level of emotional integration and sense of self was functioning at the level of a fragmented/archipelago child. This meant that although there were times when Tom could function and think about his feelings, these were very short and when faced with the slightest stress, he often broke down and fell into destructive and self-destructive behaviour.

The initial treatment programme identified the appropriate therapeutic provision and responsiveness to both his primary and secondary needs required from the team if Tom's sense of self were to develop and strengthen becoming more able to bring his thinking and feelings together.

This second assessment of Needs Led Assessment aims to discuss and review the progress that Tom has made based on the implementation of the initial therapeutic treatment programme recommended and to identify the next areas of development.

Based on observation and discussions with the team, three key areas were identified:

• **Boundaries, merging and functioning**
• **Containing emotion, anxiety, anger, and stress**
• **Communication (symbolic, verbal, and non-verbal)**

Treatment Plan dimensions	Indicate as appropriate
Boundaries, merging and functioning	X
Containing emotion, anxiety, anger, and stress	X
Self-esteem and self-preservation	

(Continued)

Communication (symbolic, verbal, and non-verbal)	X
Capacity to accept personal responsibility for their actions	
Capacity to learn from experience	
Play	
Fragile integration	

Focus of Treatment Plan

Boundaries, merging and functioning

Although Tom continues to become fragile at times. His capacity to function is stronger than before, and he is able to continue functioning positively for longer periods of time than previously. However, there are times when he becomes fragile and cannot function, placing him in danger of breaking down and possibly 'acting out' destructively. However, the positive aspect of his maturational growth and development is that Tom is now more able to ask for support and comfort from his worker when he feels fragile. This indicates that he is more able to bring his thinking and feelings together and seek help. The current outcome of the treatment programme is that the quality of attachment with some of his workers is now becoming more meaningful and stronger.

School is more difficult for him, and he finds transitions and separation difficult to manage. Tom needs a great deal of consistency if he is to continue to function in an educational setting. If there are a number of teacher changes, it prevents him from being able to think. At school, he does feel quite isolated and different from the other pupils.

Treatment programme

1 Currently, Tom requires a strong amount of emotional support from his carers. When they recognise his anxieties being expressed, either through words or with his actions, it would be helpful if they could say to him: "It seems as though you are feeling very worried at the moment, is there anything I can do to help you". Try to respond to him before it becomes too unbearable for him and which could result in him acting out or ceasing to function.

2 Help him to accept personal responsibility for his actions. As his sense of self begins to strengthen and he starts to make a meaningful attachment

with some of his workers, it will help him to build a sense of reliability and trustworthiness about his actions. The worker must focus on Tom's personal identity whilst building up and helping him to live with a sense of personal responsibility for his actions, without him feeling that he is being reacted to and attacked by the worker.

3   Although Tom is at primary school, it is inevitable that he will be faced with a school environment with pupils and teachers with whom he is not familiar. Breaks and lunchtimes are periods where there is a lot of noise and circulation of pupils who will also have friendship groups which do not include him.

It is likely that he will be based in a single classroom for most of the time with a dedicated teacher who will follow a fixed timetable. It is important to have his own support teacher who will provide a sense of familiarity and continuity and who will be able to help Tom to work through his lessons and accompany him to sessions that take place outside of his normal classroom, for example, sports activities. It will also be beneficial for Tom to have a regular place to the side of the class to sit, so that he can see around him, and for the support teacher to be given half an hour before the end of the school day, to talk with Tom to help him to review what he did and what he learnt during that day. It is important for the support teacher to work with Tom to identify areas of success for each day in addition to areas which need developing, for example, reading, what to do if he makes mistakes in his writing, and strategies for when he becomes frustrated or overwhelmed, such as mindfulness. At the end of each week, Tom and his support teacher can **together** review the progress that Tom had made during the week, e.g., the length of time he was able to concentrate on a piece of work, improvement in his writing, and the story that he had written.

Containing emotion, anxiety, anger, and stress

Tom's sense of self is strengthening, believing that the workers do hold him in their mind and think about him. However, there are still a number of times when he cannot believe in himself, so he fluctuates between idealising or denigrating himself. This means either he enjoys looking after himself, playing either in the bath or with his toys, or believing that he is a very bad person whom nobody loves. He has communicated this to his workers at times, showing his feelings by hurting himself or urinating in the bath or other places. At this point, Tom starts to disintegrate.

When he cannot value himself or feel that he is being valued by others for his actions, he feels that he cannot value himself. He feels isolated, left to his own feelings which can at times, if not recognised by the team, lead to him becoming self-destructive towards himself because he cannot look after himself properly. This can occur when his self-esteem weakens and he own sense of despair and vulnerability takes over his feelings.

Treatment programme

1 Help Tom believe that you understand how managing stress factors in his life is difficult for him and, at times, can become quite unbearable. Help him believe that you value the progress he has made and that you want to support him through to the next stage of his day-to-day living. Ask him what can you provide him with to support him.
2 When Tom presents this level of his vulnerability to others, remember, there is a part of him which presents as the small lost child that he once was, and that he still carries with him in his inner world. Reaching out to Tom could make him feel that you are nurturing him. Think of any good primary experiences he requires which could help him to feel emotionally contained by you.

Communication

Tom is currently having play therapy. This has been very helpful for him enabling him to communicate at a symbolic level. However, he is now also ready to start to communicate verbally about some his feelings. Offer as many opportunities as possible to help Tom communicate about his anxieties and fears. When he is feeling anxious and emotionally fragile, without the opportunity to communicate about how he is feeling with a worker with whom he feels safe and attached, there is a danger of breaking down and acting out once more. When you recognise the level of his anxieties, let him know that you are aware that he appears to be very worried about how he is feeling, and ask whether there is anything that you can do to help him feel safer with himself. This will help him to think about his feelings and express them through words. Tom needs to believe that he is still being held in the mind of those responsible for him.

Fragile integration

The work that the team has put in, based on the therapeutic treatment programme following the initial Needs Led Assessment, has made a positive impact on Tom. He has developed from a fragmented child to one who is moving towards a level of fragile integration. This means that he is slowly developing a sense of self which carries a meaning for him. He is slowly reaching the stage where he can make meaningful attachments with his carers and workers. However, a great deal of support and containment by the team will be needed if he is to continue to strengthen and develop his own sense of self.

Conclusion

Tom has clearly grown in terms of emotional maturational development through the team's use of Needs Led Assessments and treatment programmes during his stay at the Home. However, it is important that we recognise that any changes in his life could throw him back to his own emotional fragility. In order to help him continue with his emotional development, it is important that the team continue to write up-to-date Needs Led Assessment Programmes every few months.

Christine Bradley
Psychotherapist

Date:

CASE STUDY 2: CHARLIE (*APPROACHING FRAGILE INTEGRATION*)

NLA Proforma

Identifying and understanding the trauma experienced by the child or adolescence is the first step in creating a meaningful Needs Led Assessment and Treatment Programme. This understanding helps the team to understand the symptoms of behaviour in an unintegrated child or adolescent whose maturation and developmental processes have been disrupted because of early life experiences of trauma abandonment, abuse, and deprivation.

The outcome of the assessment is to create a treatment programme which identifies the support, communication, and provision the child or young person requires to help them to begin a process of recovery.

Needs Led Assessment and Therapeutic Treatment Programme   **Name: CHARLIE**

Name of Centre:

Name of Child: Charlie   Date:

First Needs Assessment and Treatment Plan: Yes

Background

When Charlie was born, his parents were 14 years and 15 years of age. Although he lived with them until he was four or five years old, it was a very fragmented childhood for him. He experienced a combination of feeling loved and emotionally responded to by each of them at times, whilst also having episodes of emotional and physical abuse together with episodes of hostility and aggression thrown at him. The atmosphere in which he grew up also made him feel emotionally fragile because he did not know what responses to expect when they were taking care of him. This was because although there was a good attachment relationship with both parents at times, his dependency needs were not always understood or responded to positively by them. This left Charlie feeling very afraid and unsure about himself because he did not know what to expect from them, especially as both parents were also suffering from a number of mental health difficulties.

Eventually, it was recognised by his reception class teacher that Charlie was showing signs of severe bruising on his arms. It was concluded that there was the possibility of severe physical abuse towards Charlie in the home setting. The result was that the local authority placed him into a foster home placement, which only lasted for a few days. Eventually, Charlie was placed in the Home on 3 December 2021. Although he is now very settled here, there are still a number of factors the team needs to understand about helping Charlie to manage his own internal world of emotions which are, at times, unbearable for him, causing him to act out destructively or self-destructively at times.

The team will need to set up a treatment plan which enables Charlie to function more positively, helping him develop a sense of self which becomes and feels more real to him, and which enables him to begin to think about his unbearable feelings without breaking down.

The assessment and treatment plan will help the team deepen their insight and understanding to help and support Charlie to strengthen his personal identity by developing a more positive belief within himself and his level of functioning within his day-to-day living.

Identifying the focus of the Treatment Plan

As part of the discussion, the team were asked to assess Charlie's level of integration and ego functioning, together with levels of non-functioning. From the eight key areas for development which are seen as central to the child/young person' day-to-day functioning, the team were asked to prioritise between two to four key areas.

They prioritised two areas which they felt were vital to Charlie's development and that will form the basis of the Therapeutic Treatment Programme:

- **Containing emotion, anxiety, anger, and stress**
- **Self-esteem and self-preservation**

Treatment Programme: key areas for development	Indicate as appropriate
Boundaries, merging and functioning	
Containing emotion, anxiety, anger, and stress	X
Self-esteem and self-preservation	X
Communication (symbolic, non-verbal, and verbal)	
Capacity to recover by learning from experience	
Capacity to accept responsibility for their actions	
Play	
Fragile integration	

Focus of Treatment Programme

Containing emotion, anxiety, anger, and stress

Charlie finds some aspects of his day-to-day living stressful and too difficult for him to manage. He views the reactions to his behaviour from others as being negative and attacking, which is what he internalised from his parents' behaviour towards him during the early years of his maturational development. As a result, such negative reactions towards Charlie can make him want to attack them back, often with dire circumstances. At this point, he can become overwhelmed by the pain of his internal world of emotions, which, when coupled with the stressful realities of the outside world, can become quite unbearable for him to manage. Although he can, at times, manage emotions of anxiety, anger, and stress, at other periods of the day, he can also quite easily break down when it becomes too much for him and he feels quite attacked by others. He can, at times, value good experiences in his day-to-day living; however, because he anticipates that these will break down before whatever the task that he is involved in has been completed, he tries to create a situation where it does, because he does not expect anything valuable in his life to continue.

Charlie has become very dependent on his key worker Leanne. It is crucial that he can develop a trust and belief in her that will help the relationship to become continuous for him until he can embark upon and manage the transition into developing other meaningful relationships in his day-to-day living, whether it be in the home or at school. Currently, he is moving towards functioning at the level of fragile integration. This indicates that his own sense of self is beginning to grow and strengthen. However, he is still very fragile because of the lack of continuity of good experiences in his early life, and also because of the difficulties that he has about bringing his thinking and feelings together. He cannot believe that any positive experience in his life will continue, and expects it to break down.

Charlie requires a great amount of support and provision if he is to maintain a positive belief in himself. Charlie's experience of some of his day-to-day living can place him in danger of fragmenting because he cannot hold on to a combination of both positive and negative feelings about the complexities of his day-to-day living, at the same time. This can overwhelm him with emotions which he can often find unbearable to manage, resulting in him breaking down, exhibiting difficult and negative behaviour patterns. This, in turn, can overwhelm him with emotions, which he finds unbearable to manage.

Treatment plan

Charlie is **approaching the developmental stage of fragile integration**. This means that he has acquired a sense of self which he believes in. He is, however, still very fragile, and not yet strong enough to examine and explore the realities of the outside world. He has not yet developed the capacity to believe in a sense of emotional containment from his workers. Nevertheless, it is very important to recognise that he has reached the early stages of emotional maturation. The emotionally integrated child reaches a stage where they start to make meaningful attachments with their carers. Currently, Charlie is at the starting point of developing them with others, and this is an area that the team need to be working with.

Under stress, his capacity to function could disintegrate and break down, and he could cease to function. At this stage, he requires a great deal of emotional support and provision from his carers. Let him know that you are aware that he finds life difficult at times and explain what can you provide to help him to feel and believe that you are holding him in your mind. There are times when he needs responding to and supporting like a seven-year-old, and other times, he needs the provision of a small child who feels lost. A lost small child needs to feel emotionally nurtured by his carers and workers. To prevent Charlie from acting out his unbearable feelings, it is important that the team's main task with Charlie over the next few months is to help him to think about and communicate, his negative feelings which have become unbearable and unthinkable for him.

Training required by the team

1   The provision of good primary experiences for unintegrated children and young people
2   Transference and countertransference in a therapeutic setting
3   Understanding disintegration

Self-esteem and self-preservation

As Charlie reaches a level of being more able to think about and reflect on his current experiences and the fears and anxieties that he holds about his day-to-day living, it is important to help him to understand that he cannot feel happy all the time. That way he will be able to recognise that he can recover from his unbearable feelings and move forward to functioning with a greater confidence about himself.

Fragile integration is the beginning of a sense of self with the start of ongoing attachments with others. Charlie is arriving at the starting point of attaching with meaning, to adults, but considerable therapeutic intervention needs to be undertaken with him if his sense of self is to continue to develop and strengthen.

If the team are to provide Charlie with the appropriate therapeutic intervention to help him to develop and strengthen emotionally, it is important that they are able to extend their knowledge and insight through the training suggested above.

This assessment programme informs us how the traumas, which Charlie experienced in his early years, have left him feeling unsure as to whom he belongs. What he requires from the work of the Home, his new placement, is the opportunity to reach a new starting point in his life where his own sense of self can start to develop. However, it will not be an easy task for the teachers and workers. The Needs Led Assessment that follows will inform us how the treatment plans have helped them to live alongside Charlie with his vulnerabilities and the range of survival techniques that he has developed.

Conclusion

In order for the team to provide Charlie with the appropriate therapeutic intervention to help him develop and strengthen emotionally, it is important that they receive training in the three areas proposed.

The second Needs Led Assessment is to be delivered in three months' time

Christine Bradley
Psychotherapist

Date:

Carers/Worker's Reflective Log   **Name: Charlie**

The aim of this log is to enable you to record a short reflective account following your interaction with a child or young person with whom you are working. This will help create a record that will enable you to monitor progress over time. Although you do not need to use these headings, you may find them useful as a starting point.

Name of the child/young person: Charlie	**Date:**

Summary of what took place and outcome in terms of progress (whether forward or retrograde)

- At times, workers feel as though they are making progress with Charlie, but he often becomes irritated if life does not go his way, easily becoming overwhelmed with stress.
- A worker can very often enjoy playing football with Charlie, but the slightest thing can make him angry and agitated. He finds stress often too difficult to manage.
- On his birthday, Charlie was initially very happy to see his key worker give him a gift. However, when he opened it and found it was a bike, he became very angry and told her that he hated her.
- He becomes very angry over football and cannot regulate his emotions, becoming angry and overreactive to others.
- During football games, his emotions become heightened, and he starts to hurt others even attempting to kick his carers.

- At school on his birthday, he handed over birthday sweets to the rest of the class. Because the whole class sang to him, he stood with his teacher and let her hug him. He was smiling the entire time of this experience.
- Was able to play a frisbee game without becoming overwhelmed with stress. This is a forward step for him.
- Was able to play a chess game with two others and teach the worker how to play it.
- Can play football games and keep to the rules at times.

In this section, a combination of forward and retrograde steps in his day-to-day living have been identified.

The child/young person's capacity to manage their internal world and external reality

- Charlie has difficulty managing his internal world. I have seen that it can have a negative effect on him when he is trying to manage the stresses of the external world.
- He has a limited ability to manage the stresses of the external world. At times, he withdraws from the external reality, expressing verbal frustration about his life.
- Can sometimes express his feelings but not in a calm way.
- At times, Charlie appears to be completely detached from reality. However, the worker has noticed a look of realisation, which he sometimes expresses about both himself and his behaviour.
- At times, he can show control of his own internal world and is more in touch with the pressures of reality factors in his life.
- Charlie can shut himself off from the pressures of external reality, he shuts off, and cannot accept personal responsibility for what has happened.
- Gets very frustrated when the worker is winning a game that he is playing with him.
- His behaviour escalates when he feels that other children are overreacting to him.

In this section, it is clear that Charlie has periods of both moving forwards and retrograde steps in his personality development.

Observations of child/young person's use of symbolic, verbal, and non-verbal communication

- Charlie can verbally communicate very well at times; however, when he cannot understand what I am trying to communicate, he can become non-verbal, but generally uses verbal communication well.

- Can verbalise his feelings to me, but not always in a calm way.
- Can quickly become angry and aggressive and ceases to communicate.
- Charlie is able to verbally communicate at times.
- When his emotions are very high and fragile, Charlie is able to communicate verbally, but when it is too difficult for him, he expresses himself through facial expressions.

Observation of the child/young person's emotional experience of the interaction

- At times, when I try to say goodbye to him, he either tells me to shut up or go away from him. He finds separation too painful for him to manage at times.
- Can become frustrated when he is trying something new.
- Charlie has little emotional language and finds it difficult to understand his own feelings.
- Charlie's verbal communication about his frustration is often through swearing. When he is frightened, it can come over through his face frowning and it is difficult for him to respond positively after such a reaction from him.
- At times, Charlie seems to be pleased, happy, and in control of himself.
- He wanted me to keep playing with him but was able to stop the game when I said that I needed to go.
- At times, his being upset is presented as anger.
- He became happy laughing, and he grabbed hold of my hand several times to keep me near to him.
- At times, I am unclear as to whether Charlie's emotions are ones of frustration or fear of coping with others, when he becomes excited, it is often in a negative way.

How did you feel in anticipation, prior to the interaction with the child/ young person?

- I feel that I will be received well, but sometimes he does not wish to interact with me.
- To know how to manage my day with Charlie, I always ask for a handover from staff who have been in the house all day with him.
- I can become anxious because I do not know whether Charlie's interactions with me could be a combination of emotions which mentally and emotionally I have to contain, and which I do find hard and painful at times to manage.

- I often feel anxious before a shift when I am the only worker who can manage Charlie and may not be able to spend time with other young people.
- When Charlie is playing nicely, I can be on edge, wondering when he, or if he would break down again and walk out.
- In the absence of his teacher, I wanted to distract him from being difficult and settle him, I was nervous about his reaction to the teacher not being there. Sometimes his nervousness can be presented as anger.
- I was nervous because I am aware that Charlie does not like losing a game and I was unsure about how to play it again.

How did you feel afterwards, once the interaction was over?

- I was emotional and disappointed that my interaction with him did not go better.
- I felt that my time with him had gone well and I was relieved and happy that we shared such a lovely and special moment.
- A sense of achievement and when an interaction works, I remain positive to him and thank Charlie for hanging out with me and playing.
- I can, at times, feel calm when it goes well.
- At times, I am very shaken and concerned about the well-being of the group after being with Charlie and worried about the restraint and impact of my relationship with him.
- At times, I feel really happy when it goes well.
- Often, I am emotionally exhausted and drained after spending time with Charlie.
- After difficult shifts, I am tired and drained, and also feel guilty for not giving the other children in the group the same attention I give to Charlie.
- After difficult interactions with Charlie, I can often feel defeated, sad, frustrated, and drained.
- I feel great when the interaction goes well. If it does not, I just keep being persistent because Charlie can be selective about who he wants to interact with. If I feel calm, that can have a calming influence on Charlie.

On reflection, what advice would you give yourself?

- I should have watched Charlie to pick a one-person game which I could have watched him play.
- I want to be clearer with him about his behaviour with reasons and explanations that he understands.
- I must try not to concern myself about what might go wrong but focus on the positive things which can come out of the game and my interaction with Charlie.

- I must have in my mind that there are root causes for his behaviour and try to have a better understanding of Charlie's needs.
- Try to keep presenting myself as a happy engaging person when interacting with Charlie.
- Perhaps provide Charlie with rules for the game at the start, or ask <u>him</u> for the rules.
- Take him away from the activity when he starts to be 'silly'.
- I must try not to feel anxious about him and start to trust him more.
- I often find it hard to focus on the positive aspects of Charlie's behaviour.
- Keep persistent with him and try to find different ways to engage with Charlie. Never give up and try to remember that a positive outcome can be achieved with him.
- Always be prepared to learn from those workers with more experience than me, and make sure that the knowledge of all incidents with Charlie is handed over to others.

Conclusions

This reflective log has highlighted the importance of workers being able to address their own responses and reactions about their work with Charlie. It is only by being able to reflect on their treatment and practice in their work with Charlie that they can move towards gaining a meaningful insight and understanding about helping him and other children and young people who have been seriously traumatised in their early years. This learning and insight will enable Charlie to develop and gain an emotional understanding about his day-to-day functioning and strengthen his sense of self. The reflective log can also reveal the importance of carers and workers working towards deepening their understanding about themselves and the stress and impact the work has on them personally whilst enabling them to help the children and young people for whom they are responsible to be able to manage the pain and stress they face in managing the outside world.

The Needs Led Assessments together with Therapeutic Treatment Programmes written and put into practise through the use of reflective logs, show the importance of workers taking the time to reflect on the impact that working with traumatised children and young people has on both their own emotions and professional practice. This reflection and insight help them not to act out their own emotions onto which the child can project their inner anxieties. Understanding the concept of transference and countertransference is a very important piece of training for them.

SECOND NLA PROFORMA + THERAPEUTIC   **Name: CHARLIE**
TREATMENT PROGRAMME

NLA Proforma

Identifying and understanding the trauma experienced by the child or adolescence is the first step in creating a meaningful Needs Led Assessment and Treatment Programme. This understanding helps the team to understand the symptoms of behaviour in an unintegrated child or adolescent whose maturation and developmental processes have been disrupted because of early life experiences of trauma abandonment, abuse, and deprivation.

The outcome of the assessment is to create a treatment programme which identifies the support, communication, and provision the child or young person requires to help them to begin a process of recovery.

Needs Led Assessment and Treatment Programme   **Name: CHARLIE**
Name of Centre:

Name of Child: Charlie   **Date:**

Second Needs Assessment and Therapeutic Treatment Programme

The first Needs Led Assessment and Therapeutic Treatment Programme was written three months previously. Charlie was assessed as functioning at the level of fragile integration with a sense of self at a level, which could function but easily break down under the slightest stress. This assessment will discuss the progress he has made after the team have been using the initial treatment plan. It was also agreed that in the second assessment, we would discuss and gain an insight into the use of the treatment plan, reflecting on the categories of containing emotions anxiety, anger, and stress and self-esteem, whilst also discussing play and communication.

As part of the discussion, the team were required to assess the level of integration and ego- functioning, together with levels of non-functioning of the child or adolescent, and prioritise between two to four areas which felt are vital to their development and will form the basis of the Treatment Plan. It was agreed that the focus would be on:

- **Containing emotion, anxiety, anger, and stress**
- **Communication**

Treatment Programme dimensions	Indicate as appropriate
Boundaries, merging and functioning	
Containing emotion, anxiety, anger, and stress	X
Self-esteem and self-preservation	
Communication	X
Learning from experience	
Play	
Fragile integration	

Focus of Treatment Programme

Containing emotion, anxiety, anger, and stress

Since the last assessment and treatment plan, the team acknowledge that they are now more insightful about the depth of the feelings that Charlie has to deal with. Charlie lives with feelings of loneliness and of constantly being scared. His fear is that if he attaches to a team member, they will start to hate him as he believes that his mother does. The team's use of the treatment programme and their work on holding Charlie in their minds have helped him to become more aware that the team **do** think about him. Their work has helped Charlie to begin to express his emotions. He fluctuates between being able to express his feelings and allowing the team to discuss it with him, to becoming overwhelmed with emotions of rage and despair which he cannot yet think about. These feelings are too raw for him. This results in Charlie's behaviour becoming quite aggressive and unable to accept personal responsibility for his actions. As the team are now more in touch with Charlie and the complexities of his inner world, their work has become more painful for them. This should be taken as a sign of good therapeutic treatment taking place through their work with him. It also highlights the importance of them needing to receive more training about understanding the concept of transference and countertransference in a therapeutic relationship.

Charlie is a highly intelligent child. Both the team and Charlie are aware of his need to make meaningful attachments with them, which he so desperately would like to achieve. However, because he is so afraid that if he becomes dependent on one person, they will move towards not wanting him and he will continue to feel rejected. This has led him to develop what is known as a 'false self' where he pretends to others that all is well with him, whilst at the same time, the real self is filled with internal struggles and fears about the outside world attacking him. This can lead Charlie to being in danger of acting out his fears and despair about whether he can manage his capacity to function in the outside world.

Although the work has become more painful for the team, they are working well with Charlie and developing their insight and understanding about the inner world of Charlie. They do also now realise that if they are to reach a new starting point in the maturational development of Charlie, they are going to have to help him to work through some of the most painful feelings which he carries with him. Importantly, Charlie is now also working towards being able to communicate his fears and uncertainties to the team.

Communication

Charlie is gaining the capacity to communicate verbally, and at times, he can use words to express his fears and anxieties. He is also receiving play therapy on a weekly basis, which is helpful to him. However, because Charlie is so intelligent, he does also now need to learn how to turn some of his play into verbal communication. This will enable him to start to turn his feelings into thinking and begin the process of working through verbally some of his most unbearable thoughts and feelings.

Therapeutic Treatment Programme

There are two areas on which to focus:

1   When the team becomes aware that Charlie's anxieties and uncertainties are expressed through his actions and his manic behaviour, it is important to show that you recognise this. Say to him "I know that you are feeling anxious and uncertain about what is going on - Is there anything I can do to help you to feel more aware of what is happening". Although this will be rather painful for the team, it must take place in order to help Charlie feel that he is listened to, and importantly, heard by you.
2   Additional training for the team in the areas is listed below. These will enable the team to provide Charlie with the therapeutic understanding that he requires to enable his sense of self to strengthen and become more real, both to himself and others:

- **Transference and countertransference in a therapeutic setting**
- **Making sense of symbolic communication**
- **Verbal and non-verbal communication in children and young people**

Both Needs Led Assessment and Therapeutic Treatment Plans on Charlie identify the importance of workers becoming more insightful and developing an understanding about the impact that therapeutic treatment plans have in their work with traumatised children and young people and about their meaningful work they have achieved in developing the capacity to understand and respond to meeting the child/young person's emotional needs.

Conclusion

This case study has illustrated the importance of carers/workers being able to follow the advice and guidance of the treatment programme if they are to reach the true identity of the 'real self' in a traumatised child. The carers/workers have become more aware of the times when **they** themselves require significant emotional provision, and times when strong emotional support is required from them, enabling the child to manage the pressures of meeting the demands of external reality whilst also, and importantly, feeling held in the mind of those who are responsible for them.

This follow-up Needs Led Assessment and Therapeutic Treatment Programme has also evidenced the painful reflections experienced by workers when they start to become more in touch with the sense of self and a deeper understanding about how feelings of hopelessness and helplessness in the child's inner world affect their capacity to function positively. It is important to reflect and think about what this means not only for the child but also for the worker themselves. This is the start of a meaningful and true therapeutic treatment being provided for traumatised children and young people, and as Barbara Dockar-Drysdale pointed out in 1975, "there is a difference between good child care and therapeutic management", a point that is as relevant today as it was then.

Follow-up Needs Led Assessment date for next meeting: to be confirmed

Christine Bradley
Psychotherapist

Date:

CASE STUDY 3: GEORGE (FRAGILE INTEGRATED)

FIRST NEEDS LED ASSESSMENT + THERAPEUTIC TREATMENT PROGRAMME: GEORGE (FRAGILE INTEGRATED)

Identifying and understanding the trauma experienced by the child or adolescence is the first step in creating a meaningful Needs Led Assessment and Treatment Programme. This understanding helps the team to understand the symptoms of behaviour in an unintegrated child or adolescent whose maturation and developmental processes have been disrupted because of early life experiences of trauma abandonment, abuse, and deprivation.

The outcome of the assessment is to create a treatment programme which identifies the support, communication, and provision the child or young person requires to help them to begin a process of recovery.

Needs Led Assessment + Therapeutic Treatment Programme   **Name: GEORGE**
Name of Centre:

Name of Child: George	**Date:**
Team Present: 1 Clinical psychologist 2 Director of the residential setting 3 Assistant manager 4 Christine Bradley Consultant Psychotherapist 5 Registered manager	

First Needs Assessment and Treatment Programme: Yes

Step 1: observation

George was with his family until he was six years of age. His parents separated, and his mother met another partner who moved in with them and with whom she had other children. She had miscarried a child before George and then had three more children as well as George, one before he was born and two at a later date. There was great neglect within the family and reports of possible sexual abuse between the other siblings. Although the mother was quite bonded with George it was difficult to identify the quality of their relationship because she did not show ongoing natural warmth towards him. It has been stated that after George had received a visit from his mother, he became angry and defiant to both adults and children after she left him. The ambivalent relationship that he had with his mother did not allow George to make a natural transition from her because she was not able to maintain a positive sense of emotional containment between them.

Step 2: identifying the focus of the Therapeutic Treatment Programme

As part of the discussion, the team are required to assess the level of integration and ego functioning, together with levels of non-functioning of the child or adolescent, and prioritise between two to four areas which felt are vital to their development and will form the basis of the Treatment Plan.

Given the complex situation, of the eight key areas for development, it was agreed to prioritise the following two areas:

• **Containing emotions, anxiety, anger, and stress**
• **Communication**

Treatment Programme: key areas for development	Indicate as appropriate
Self-esteem and self-preservation	
Containing emotion, anxiety, anger, and stress	X
Boundaries, merging and functioning	
Communication	X
Learning from experience and education	
Capacity to anticipate	
Play	
Fragile integration	

Focus of Treatment Programme

Containing emotion, anxiety, anger, and stress: observation

George is in danger of acting out angry feelings, which he cannot communicate other than physically, and then becomes overwhelmed by them. This is particularly so after he has had a meeting with his mother. If not worked through and supported by his carers, he is in danger of becoming potentially violent to others. However, with support and help from his carers, he can work through the emotions he carries with him relating to his sense of loss about his mother. He finds it very difficult to communicate verbally about how he feels. Although he desperately would like to have a sense of receiving greater meaningful contact with his mother, he finds separation very difficult, and this can result in him feeling deeply disappointed when his expectations of meeting her do not materialise. George is a deeply emotionally fragile child, whose sense of self is raw.

He is functioning at the level of a **fragile integrated child**, so he has developed a sense of self which he is attempting to live with. Although he did receive aspects of good parenting from his mother, the parenting was inconsistent and linked with chaotic times living with her. George does not present as coming together as a whole person. He is very emotionally fragile, and at times, he can start to break down and act out destructively or self-destructively. His inner world is filled with both negative and positive feelings, which can either support him to function or can lead him to giving up on any sense of hopefulness about his life. It is crucial that workers can recognise that George does carry some very intense negative feelings about himself and others.

George requires a great deal of emotional support from his carers, but he does have the capacity to work through and learn from his painful experiences, which, at times, will be as painful for workers as it will be for George to manage. There is a part of him which has always felt isolated, on his own with his emotions. If the carers can show that they hold the feelings of George in their mind, he will not feel as isolated and alone as he did before.

George finds being on his own difficult because he has always felt isolated and he believes that nobody wants to be with him. It will be an important although painful piece of work for the team to help George believe that they can hold him in their mind when they cannot be with him. In time, it is hoped that George will be able to believe that he does matter to others.

Communication: observation

George is able to communicate verbally at times; however, when reality becomes too stressful for him, he becomes emotionally raw and is in danger of breaking down and falling into anti-social behaviour because he feels so fragile. At this point, his sense of self starts to disintegrate, and he loses signs of hope for himself, so in danger of being consumed with feeling of hopelessness and helplessness about facing and managing the demands of the reality of the outside world.

Step 3: therapeutic treatment Programme

George is functioning at the level of a fragilely integrated child. This means that he has developed a sense of self which he is struggling to live with, and although he did receive some aspects of good parenting from his mother, they were so intermittent and at times chaotic. Currently, he is functioning at the level of an **emotionally fragile child**, and at times of stress, he can fall apart and begin to break down and act out, either destructively or self-destructively. George's inner world is filled with both negative and positive feelings, which can either support him to function or lead to him giving up any sense of hopefulness about his life. We must recognise that George's inner world carries some very intense and at times negative feelings.

He requires a great deal of emotional support from his carers, although he does have the capacity to work through and learn from some of his most painful experiences. At times, this will be as painful for the workers as it will be for George to manage. It is important to acknowledge that there is a part of him which has always felt on his own with his feelings.

Containing emotion, anxiety, anger, and stress: guidance

George needs to believe that those caring for him in the Home are holding him in their mind. Although there are times when George appears to be coming together as a person, he is not yet emotionally strong enough to manage difficult and painful times in his day-to-day living. To strengthen his sense of self, he needs to believe that those caring for him are holding him together, so enabling him to be able to bear some of the most difficult times in the day. Help him to see that sometimes going through the most painful times of his day can result in him feeling stronger about himself.

George needs some help to bring his thinking and feelings together, which will to support him to strengthen his ego development. He has now reached a stage where child psychotherapy could be beneficial for him to enable him to start to communicate about some of his most painful feelings.

Communication: guidance

When George's sense of self starts to become fragile, it may be helpful to move him over to some form of symbolic communication through play or something creative to help prevent him from 'acting out' destructively or self-destructively as he is not yet able to express himself through words.

Offer as many opportunities as possible to help George communicate about the stress he finds about facing reality factors in his day-to-day living. Express your concern when you see him not being able to communicate about his anxieties and is in danger of breaking down. Ask if there is anything you can do to help him. This way he will feel that you are holding him in your mind.

Discuss with the team the use of play opportunities for him as a means of communication.

The long-term aim of therapeutic work with George is to help his sense of self to strengthen and more able to manage the demands of managing the external reality factors in his life.

Training points for workers:

In discussion with the team and given the complexity of George's background, it is suggested that the following three areas would help develop workers' knowledge and skills:

- **Transference and countertransference in a therapeutic setting**
- **The provision of good primary experience**
- **Integration and unintegration**

Conclusion

George is characterised as being **fragilely integrated**, which means that his sense of self is stronger than it is in other syndromes of deprivation. He is capable of managing stress factors but for a short period only. His emotional resources are not yet strong enough to help him hold onto his self-esteem continually, and without support, his resources can easily disintegrate. It is anticipated that with the use of the treatment programme, George's sense of self will start to strengthen.

The team have now identified the lost parts of George. Although he can communicate and seeks strong attachments from others, the team will have to work hard to convince him that adults are holding him in their mind so that he can begin to understand that he can hold onto an attachment relationship with it without it breaking down. The next NLA will take place in three months' time and will also include the team completing the reflective log.

A follow-up meeting is to be held in November.

Christine Bradley
Psychotherapist

Date:

Carer/Worker Reflective Log   **Name: George**

The aim of this log is to enable you to record a short reflective account following your interaction with a child or young person with whom you are working. This will help create a record that will enable you to monitor progress over time. Although you do not need to use these headings, you may find them useful as a starting point.

Name of the child/young person: George   **Date:**

Summary of what took place and outcome in terms of progress (whether forward or retrograde)

1 The worker and one member of staff spent time playing with George after tea. This is the first time that he was able to play with workers without using electronic tablets, or other electronic objects. *This is a huge progress in him.* His capacity to function is becoming stronger daily.

2 For the first time, he went swimming with a new residential worker. It went well and he enjoyed it. This is the first time George has gone swimming without the particular worker on whom he was dependent. After a night's sleep, George woke up early and spoke about a nightmare that he had during the night. *This is a very positive way forward for him,* being able to communicate more about his dream, a sign that he is becoming more in touch with his emotions, fears, and anxieties and is able to communicate about them to his workers. Whilst playing a board game with others George is now more able to regulate his emotions than previously. If he did not win the game before, he would have reacted badly with aggressive behaviour. However, on this occasion, he laughed and joined in with the team members and carried on playing. *This is a very positive way forward for him.*

3 During a visit to the bowling alley, he was told to stop trying to pass a very heavy ball around, placing other children in danger of being hit by the ball. On his return after being out of the alley for a short period, he noticed that one of his peers was trying to control the situation. In spite of this, George continued trying to control the actions of his peer until the game ended. *This is a big sign that he is beginning to accept personal responsibility for his actions.*

In this section, there are strong signs of forward steps in George's emotional development.

The child/young person's capacity to manage their internal world and external reality

1 George is now more able to regulate his emotions than previously. This is a result of the assessment and treatment plan being used by the workers. This is illustrated by when he was being encouraged not to pass the bowls to other children, this did not result in any physical behaviours being acted out by him. Previously, this would have resulted in him becoming challenging, refusing to follow instructions, and expressing verbal dissatisfaction at being asked not to move the balls.
2 After playing a game with two workers, previously he had to cheat in order to win. Today, he played the game correctly and accepted it when other people won. This is a proof that George is being able to accept personal responsibility for his behaviour and is thinking about the rest of the group that he is playing with.
3 He appeared confused one morning after his nightmare and spoke about the wolf in his dream and how frightened he was of it.
4 After personal contact with his mother, he was very positive about the time that he spent with her and explained how he had enjoyed his time with her. George had previously not been able to experience contact with his mother so positively. *This is a forward-thinking development for him.*

Observations of child/young person's use of symbolic, verbal, and non-verbal communication

1 During the games he was playing and using a ball, it was clear that George was more able to communicate his frustrations. Previously, when a staff member was in the lead of the game, he would make aggressive comments such as "you are cheating". However, currently, it seems that his aggressive verbalisation has softened and he can communicate to the workers non-verbally through smiling and laughing throughout the game. At the end of the game, he asked for a hug from a worker before going to bed.
2 When George was visiting his mother, he was visibly happy when he was collected by his residential worker. She noticed that he was smiling and laughing with his mum and hugging her very tightly. *This signifies another positive way forward in George's emotional growth and development.*
3 Whilst waiting for his turn in bowling, he kept playing with the bowls. Staff suggested to him that he should put them down in order to help him

not feel the urgency of picking up a bowl. Although he did not verbalise his anger and displeasure at being asked to stop the action, it was communicated non-verbally through his body action and stance. *Importantly, however, there was no acting out from him.*

4   When George spoke about his dream, he spoke openly about it and described about what happened in detail. *This is a very good positive sign showing that he is starting to be clearer about his need to communicate and express some of his own fears and uncertainties.*

Observation of the child/young person's emotional experience of the interaction

1   George was very happy whilst playing the game and seemed to enjoy the interaction between himself and the workers.

2   Prior to collecting George from his mother's, the worker noticed that he was a little apprehensive about him being in her personal car. In the past, he has not always behaved in a positive manner in vehicles and certainly not after contact with his mother. The worker experienced being with him to and from his mother, as a huge growth change in his attitude towards herself and his mother. This means that George is changing himself emotionally, hopefully feeling a little stronger about himself.

3   The worker noticed that George was happy whilst playing a game and appeared to enjoy the interaction between himself and the worker. Such positive interaction from him is a new response from him. *This is a very positive reaction.*

4   During a period of time that he spent with a worker, George appeared to be happy throughout the interaction and smiled whilst being able to relinquish control for that period of time, allowing himself to be taken care of by the worker. *A very new and positive interaction.*

How did you/the worker feel in anticipation, prior to the interaction with the child/young person?

W1   Prior to collecting George from his mothers in her own car for the first time, the worker was a little apprehensive about him being in her own personal car. However, he asked many questions about the car and how it worked. During the journey, he behaved in a very positive manner and thanked her for the journey. *It was the first time that he behaved well after a visit to his mother's house.*

Observation:

The worker who collected George from his mother's was very pleased with the outcome. He behaved perfectly in her car, which had not occurred before. He was also very positive about being a passenger in the car. He said that he enjoyed the journey. This is also a sign that George is becoming more able to take in good experiences from his workers. *This is very good progress on his part.*

W2   The worker anticipated playing the board game and was looking forward to spending time with George, and she found it enjoyable being able to spend some quality time with him.

Observation:

Playing board games consistently with him cannot always offer a positive experience, because he can be very upset if he does not win the game. However, if the team can hold the positive potential of George in their mind, and use a playful tone with him throughout the game, they will offer a positive model of working with him and provide a good role model for George. This will result in him starting to copy this playful interaction. Although the team does also recognise that he is not always successful, they must also help George to recognise that positive approaches need to be played out and are part of the game. Prior to the game that they played, the worker was not looking forward to or anticipating a positive outcome, because it had been some time since he had played a game with George, and it was always in the back of his mind whether George would engage with him or not and become difficult to manage. The fear was that if George did not win, he would create aggressive arguments.

How did you feel afterwards, once the interaction was over?
W1   The worker was really pleased with the outcome of the journey. She experienced a very different response from him, in a car after being with his mother. This is a sign that George is starting to develop emotionally in his day-to-day living and be able to think about more painful experiences and the effect this has on him.
W2   He was really very pleased with the outcome. The worker observed that George enjoyed the game and so did the team who were playing with him. He was very pleased and felt reassured to see George following the rules and accepting that he did not always have to win.

W3 The worker was very pleased that George could speak openly to him rather than acting out his feelings. The worker felt happy and satisfied that George told him that he had enjoyed the time that he spent with both staff members. They were relieved that the game had ended well and did not escalate into negative behaviour as had happened in the past. This gives them strong signs that George is strengthening his own sense of self, making it more possible for him to function positively.

On reflection, what advice would you give yourself?

1 On reflection, I would advise myself not to begin an activity with George thinking that it may result in negative behaviour, because of the numerous times that it has ended like that in the past. I am more aware that thinking positively about George is far more beneficial when building up a thera-peutic relationship with him, rather than thinking about it in a negative manner. Current work with him is proving that this is a true statement. Unconditional positive regard for George will strengthen the therapeutic alliance with him and allow for greater growth and development in him.
2 To continue to engage with George and listen to what he has to say to me when playing with and learn how to respond to him appropriately.
3 I am starting to believe that George will not always behave like he did in the past. I must be far more aware and insightful as to how much he has changed over the past months.
4 I will continue to listen to George as he is now starting to become more open in his communication.

SECOND NLA PROFORMA + THERAPEUTIC TREATMENT PROGRAMME   Name: GEORGE

NLA Proforma

Identifying and understanding the trauma experienced by the child or adolescence is the first step in creating a meaningful Needs Led Assessment and Treatment Programme. This understanding helps the team to understand the symptoms of behaviour in an unintegrated child or adolescent whose maturation and develop-mental processes have been disrupted because of early life experiences of trauma abandonment, abuse, and deprivation.

The outcome of the assessment is to create a treatment programme, which identi-fies the support, communication, and provision the child or young person requires to help them to begin a process of recovery.

Name of Child: George   **Date:**

This is the second Needs Assessment and Therapeutic Treatment Programme

In the initial Needs Led Assessment George was assessed as functioning at the level of a **fragilely integrated child**. This meant that although he experienced several traumatic experiences in his earlier life, they were also combined with a mixture of episodes of good nurturing from his primary carers. This has helped George to develop a stronger and more real sense of self, which he can, at times, feel comfortable with, and which allows him to function positively.

However, George continues to remain emotionally fragile, which means that the stress factors he has to face in his day-to-day living can become, at times, quite unbearable for him to manage and can lead to him acting out his feelings destructively or aggressively. To help him, the team needs to identify a range of appropriate responses and the emotional support that will make him feel supported enough so that he can work towards bringing his thinking and feelings together and begin to understand why his behaviour has become too difficult for him to manage. This assessment and treatment programme will examine the development of George's maturational growth and development, which will enable him to strengthen his own sense of self.

The initial diagnosis dimensions listed below are central to the child or adolescent's day-to-day living. They comprise:

1   Boundaries, merging and functioning
2   Containing emotions of anxiety, anger, and stress
3   Self-esteem and self-preservation
4   Communication
5   Learning from experience
6   Play
7   Fragile integration

As part of the discussion, the team were required to assess the level of integration and ego functioning, together with levels of non-functioning of George, and prioritise between two to four areas which felt were vital to his development and will form the basis of the Treatment Plan.

The following two areas have been identified by the team and are examined below:

- **Containing emotion, anxiety, anger, and stress**
- **Learning from experience**

Treatment Plan dimensions	Indicate as appropriate
Boundaries, merging and functioning	
Containing emotion, anxiety, anger, and stress	X
Self-esteem and self-preservation	
Communication	
Learning from experience	X
Play	
Fragile integration	

Focus of Treatment Programme

Containing emotion, anxiety, anger, and stress

Since the last assessment and treatment programme George's behaviour has, regressed, in that at times he becomes aggressive and quite destructive. However, he is also showing signs that with support from the team, he can return to his more positive levels of functioning and is willing at times to apologise for his behaviour.

The team have identified the part of his life and behaviour as being difficult for them to emotionally contain and this relates to change. The basis of this behaviour lies in George's response to what is happening in the Home. There have been some changes in the Home, and they recognise that George finds managing change and the making of transitions too painful and difficult for him to manage. This is mainly because a boy in the home with whom George could relate to positively was leaving his placement. George finds the absence and loss of a person whom he enjoyed being with difficult and painful to manage. This leads back to earlier memories of him receiving good experiences from his mother but losing them before he could internalise these positive memories. As a consequence, he is unable to integrate and think about the importance of good experiences in his life with good memories that he can hold onto. Instead, George continues to expect any good experiences which he receives to break down before he has been able to hold them in his mind.

At school, George is struggling and finds it very difficult being part of his peer group activities. He seems to become so anxious about interacting positively with the group. In order to prevent him from acting out aggressively towards them, and stopping the group from functioning positively in their lessons, he has been placed on a table on his own for lessons. This has made him feel more isolated and alone. However, although he regresses back to a more infantile behaviour, it is important to note that after a period of ten minutes, George apologises to the teacher and starts to function in his lesson again.

Learning from Experience

After the team's use of the therapeutic treatment programme based on the previous assessment, George is now showing that although he continues to break down when under stress, he is now more able to repair his relationship with his workers, becoming more engaging and more able to reflect on his behaviour than previously. Consequently, George is becoming more able to learn from his experiences and to think about his behaviour. When he feels that his behaviour has broken down, he can now start to show signs that he can attempt to repair himself and his relationships.

Although it is also acknowledged that there still remains some considerable emotional pain and turmoil in him, he is now approaching a stage where sessions of child psychotherapy could be helpful for enabling him to think about his emotions and how he can manage them.

Though George's level of functioning remains at a stage of fragile integration, his levels of functioning are strengthening, and he is beginning to think about himself when under stress. In time, this could help him move towards the stage of integration with his own sense of self-strengthening, and become more meaningful for him in his day-to-day living.

The following treatment programme needs to be delivered by the team:

Attachment and dependency

As George starts to become more attached to workers at the Home, it is important that you identify when his levels of functioning require additional support from you, and particularly when he requires providing for, like a small child. In order to help him manage transitions from home to school and learn how to manage the different environments that he is involved in, help George to believe that you are thinking about him even when you are not with him. This will help him to understand that you are holding him in your mind. He will then become more able to internalise the experiences that he is trying to manage and his own sense of self starts to function. Slowly, he will begin to function more positively as he becomes more in touch with his own inner world without becoming overwhelmed by his emotions.

Fantasy and reality

When George begins to express a level of high anxiety, help him to understand the difference between the actual reality factors he is having to face, and the feelings that he carries with him that surface because of previous experiences. If he is hanging onto internal stress and anxiety from previous experiences in his life, help him to believe that what he is having to manage currently is <u>very different</u> than the painful times he has experienced in the past.

Transitional objects

The team should think about certain small objects which matter to George, which he could carry with him during the day and which he could hold onto when is left feeling overwhelmed with anxiety. This could help him to feel more secure when facing certain reality factors that he has to manage, for example, when in school.

It is clear from the two assessments and treatment plans that because of the therapeutic treatment plans that the team have put into place, George is starting to build up a sense of self that he is becoming more secure with, even though he remains emotionally fragile at times. To help him to continue to emotionally strengthen his own sense of self, so that he can manage both fantasy and reality factors in his life, the team should continue with follow-up assessments and treatment programme twice a year, together with the reflective logs to record how the team's relationship with George develops.

Follow-up Needs Led Assessment and Therapeutic Treatment Programme

A follow-up assessment and treatment programme for George should be held in six months' time. It is anticipated that because of the use of the treatment programme, George is reaching a stage of inner security and developing a stronger sense of self.

Christine Bradley
Psychotherapist

Date:

The four Case studies that follow of Amy, Jimmy, Jessica, and Kiera comprise Needs Led Assessments and Therapeutic Treatment Plans with an accompanying update of the young person's progress and development.

CASE STUDY OF AMY (FROZEN)

This is the second Assessment and Therapeutic Treatment Programme   **Date:**

In the previous Needs Led Assessment on Amy held six months previously, she was described as having made a great deal of progress in her emotional growth and development over the previous months. Previously, she was assessed as functioning at the level of a frozen child, who had been so traumatised at an early stage of her emotional development that she was not able to think about her emotions and learn from them, because she found it too painful. The therapeutic work brought into practise by her workers resulted in Amy being able to function at the level of fragile ego integration, and she reached a stage of emotional development from where a sense of self which she could live with is evolving, and having attained a certain level of acceptance and awareness about herself as a person in her own right. At times of stress, she could 'disintegrate' and fall apart for a short while when her emotions became too unbearable for her to manage. However, since that time, and because the Home has been following the therapeutic treatment plan, Amy is now internalising a sense of self which she believes to be real in her and is starting to develop a 'secure base' from which she can develop emotionally. She is now more able to learn from her experiences, which can bring out both positive and negative emotions in her. At times of stress, her level of self-esteem can become very fragile and she can easily experience feelings of worthlessness and hopelessness. At this stage of her day-to-day living, Amy needs a great deal of psychological and physical reassurance from her workers, if she is to return back to feelings of hope about managing her day-to-day living experiences.

Focus of Treatment Programme

To assess her level of integration and ego functioning, together with Amy's areas of functioning and non-functioning, three key areas were identified by the team as providing the focus to her treatment plan:

- **Boundaries, merging and functioning**
- **Self-esteem and self-preservation**
- **Communication stays in**

Q1. Can Amy hold onto boundaries, but push them in an anti-authority way?

Amy's sense of self is beginning to strengthen; at school, she is managing to take part in activities at a number of different levels, including music and other creative activities. However, she continues to find transitions difficult to manage, and under stress can easily fall into a pattern of emotional disintegration. Without strong support from her workers, she can break down either through her behaviour being acted out destructively or self-destructively or by Amy retreating into herself and becoming isolated. There are elements of Amy's day-to-day living which can lead her into experiencing the management of reality as being quite unbearable at times.

Q2. Under stress does she lack self-esteem and self-preservation; can she become self-destructive?

Amy's self-esteem is still fragile and at times she can feel worthless and hopeless about herself. To survive, she needs a great deal of reassurance from the workers through their commitment and continual support which is meaningful towards her at times of stress. Amy's sense of self and personal identity is not yet strong enough to protect herself from the stress factors she experiences when she is managing certain reality factors in her day-to-day living. She needs constant reassurance from her carers when she feels overwhelmed with anxiety, because her sense of personal identity both personally and psychologically is still quite fragile and in its early stages. She can easily become confused as to where she is and to whom she belongs. However, she is now beginning to make significant attachment relationships with certain workers in the Home. Although this is a very important step in her emotional development and personal growth, it is important for workers to recognise that there could be some difficult times ahead for Amy as she becomes more aware of her own sense of self and what it brings up for her about past experiences of trauma and hostility.

Therapeutic treatment programme arising from Questions 1 and 2

Disintegration

Amy needs considerable emotional support if her level of emotional integration is to strengthen. If the outside world feels too much for her and she is in a state of disintegration, she could begin to see the outside world as a threatening place to be a part of. It is important at this stage that when her workers are aware that she is feeling overwhelmed by the pressures of the outside world, to respond to her accordingly, helping her to realise that they are in touch with her unbearable emotions. Help her to find a safe place she can be in in the Home where she can be with herself reflecting on her current situation either with a carer she trusts and relies on or on her own. Help her to retreat to her own inner world with a sense of safety and trust.

Hopelessness and hope

Reaching a stage of emotional integration is a huge achievement for Amy and her carers. She is reaching a greater awareness of herself as a person, but this can also bring up feelings of Amy's own sense of worthlessness. Although she is now using her individual therapy well, there is still a need for workers at the Home to understand that as she continues to strengthen her sense of self, it could bring up some depression in her. It is important that workers view her depression as a sign of hope as she becomes more aware of her own emotions. Even though her therapy will continue to help her through her feelings of loss and grief, she will continue to need ongoing support from her workers. Amy needs support to help her recognise that you value what she is achieving, even though it is feeling awful for her at times, realising that often it can be a positive way forward, if she is to feel strong enough to find her place in reality which is manageable and bearable for her.

Transference and countertransference

As Amy starts to experience herself as a separate person in her own right through her individual psychotherapy, she will become more in touch with some of her earlier feelings, and could at times transfer onto her workers feelings of anxiety and uncertainty, anger, and rage. These emotions in her often belong to previous unresolved traumas and negative experiences from her earlier life. It could be that the thought patterns she holds onto about previous traumas and fears of abandonment have been internalised, which under stress could be transferred onto the worker. Without appropriate intervention and workers' understanding about their own transference relationship with Amy this could result in their reacting inappropriately towards her day-to-day living experiences and thus creating more acting out either destructively or self-destructively. Workers need to be constantly reflective on what their time with Amy has brought up **for them** when their work with her has been completed. There is also a need for a reflective process within the team about their current encounters with Amy.

Q2. Communication

Amy is beginning to express herself verbally but is still more open to symbolic communication. She is very positive about her psychotherapy with her key worker and uses it well. As she becomes more confident and feels safe in the Home, her capacity to communicate symbolically is easier for her. Amy can use verbal communication when she allows her emotions to be expressed but needs to feel that workers understand what she is trying to express.

Therapeutic Treatment Plan

Use Amy's symbolic communication through play or other creative activities to enable her to express emotions and thoughts which she cannot express in any other way. Work towards understanding her expression of the symbols and what they represent about Amy's thoughts and ideas which she cannot express verbally. Recognise it when she does find the words to express how she is feeling and value them for her.

Conclusion

The team have helped Amy to make some highly significant movements in her emotional growth and development during her period of stay in the home. The therapeutic practice they have used, together with the use of the therapeutic treatment programme, has helped Amy to move from a state of unintegration to ego-integration (coming together as a person), with a sense of self and ready to make meaningful attachment relationships with workers.

However, there is still some way to go with her she will continue to need support and provision for some time to come if she is to internalise her stay at the Home when she eventually is ready to move on.

Key factors for the team to discuss in the care and treatment of Amy:

1 Managing separations and transitions
2 Opportunities for communication verbal and symbolic

Update on Amy's progress and development:

Two years later, following the work that I originally carried out with the Home, I enquired how Amy was progressing. I was informed that her placement had broken down shortly after her previous Needs Led Assessment Programme had been written.

On reflection, it was clear that the manager and part of the team did not have the opportunity either through professional development or the use of reflective log to have an opportunity to reflect and gain insight into the level of their relationships with Amy and the evidence of transference and countertransference that existed between Amy and the workers, which they were unable to disengage themselves from.

Shortly after the NLA had been written, she developed a strong dependency relationship with the teaching assistant at her school who also became strongly attached to Amy. What had not been recognised was that Amy had not yet reached the stage where she could make meaningful attachments with adults, and where she was able to accept personal responsibility for her behaviour. There was a small child in Amy who had become a 'false self' in her relationship to others, where she presented herself as functioning well but the slightest stress in her day led her to act out at times quite violently. The foster placement lasted only a few months, at which point she went back to live with her mother.

After a short period on her return to live with her mother, Amy's new school placement broke down. No one has made contact with her original placement, and therefore it has not been possible for the team to know the outcome for Amy.

Following the assessment and treatment programme, the following points should have been highlighted as a priority Amy's ability to manage transitions should have been discussed.

1 What separation and loss meant to Amy and the kind of support she needed in order to manage this.
2 The team needed to have a deeper understanding about Amy's ability to manage experiences of separation and loss in her life.
3 The use of reflective logs by the team may have helped them to develop a deeper understanding about their relationship with Amy.
4 The team need to have a deeper understanding about the sense of self in emotionally fragile children and young people.

CASE STUDY OF JIMMY *(FRAGMENTED/ARCHIPELAGO)*

Jimmy lived with his birth family for the first four years of his life. During this period, he was exposed to a number of disturbing and traumatic episodes including alcoholism, drugs, aggression, violence, constant neglect, and emotional privation. At the age of four years, he was fostered with his two older siblings to whom he was very attached. After one year, Jimmy and his sisters were both adopted by different families. The two siblings together, and Jimmy on his own not only because he was younger than his siblings, but because he had been more deeply traumatised by his birth parents. It was felt that he initially required a deeper experience of maternal nurturing from his adoptive mother than his sisters. The result of his early trauma is that he remains a deeply vulnerable and fragmented young person who is emotionally fragile, unable to think about his feelings and what it means to him when he is overwhelmed with emotions of panic and rage which can so easily become acted out by him often with destructive consequences.

Jimmy was adopted at the age of five years through a single-parent adoption. He was experienced by the adoptive mother as functioning on two levels, at times delightful and warm to be with, but at other times prone to fits of fury which were characterised by emotions of panic, rage, and aggression towards her. Unbearable anxiety in the form of panic and rage can erupt without reason in a child who has been traumatised and has no secure attachment. Without help and support it can become impossible for them to accept personal responsibility for their behaviour.

In contrast, a five-year-old who has experienced a secure attachment with their parent figure, when under pressure, is more likely to express their anxiety in the form of a temper tantrum from which they can explain their reasoning and use it to learn from as their own sense of self develops and strengthens. The difference is that the anger and frustration expressed by Jimmy is very different and emerges from panic and rage. The former can be thought about, whilst Jimmy's panic and rage is so deeply embedded in his mind that it is difficult and painful to help him communicate his emotions and so the pain remains too unbearable for him to think about.

Jimmy is now 12 years of age and has been with the adoptive mother for the past six years. The adoptive mother and her wider family remain totally committed to Jimmy and his placement with her, but she is also deeply concerned about his capacity to function appropriately during his journey into adolescence. Any stress factor in his day-to-day living leads to him becoming socially and emotionally isolated. Although he remains deeply attached and absolutely dependent on his mother, he finds it almost impossible to be separated from her, and he continues to experience the outside world as being almost impossible to manage. Jimmy's emotional state of functioning remains at the level of the lost, isolated, and abused infant he had been.

I met Jimmy once briefly after I had met the adoptive mother. I experienced him as a delightful young person but who was also emotionally fragile. In discussion with the mother, the three areas of the emotional Needs Led

Assessment Programme which would focus the treatment plan for Jimmy were as follows:

- **Containing emotion, anxiety, anger, and stress**
- **Self-esteem and self-preservation**
- **Separation and loss, managing transitions**

Containing emotion, anxiety, anger, and stress

Since his adoption, Jimmy's behaviour fluctuates between presenting himself as being charming and engaging, but the slightest stress factor in his day-to-day living results in aggressive and violent episodes, which causes him to behave destructively or self-destructively. This can be very difficult and painful for his adoptive mother to manage.

Although she has been able to manage such episodes of acting out, at times, it has been very painful for her to hold onto Jimmy without over-reacting to his behaviour negatively. Nevertheless, after a period of time of him living with his adoptive mother in her home, he became more able to apologise for his behaviour. Jimmy has a fragile sense of self, and he cannot cope with any sense of loss in his day-to-day living. An example of this is his extreme fears and worries that his mother may die or disappear when he is not with her. Although he has developed a strong attachment to his adoptive mother, he has not been able to develop a sense of self which he feels comfortable with as an individual in his own right. Since he has suffered such intense early trauma, he still needs to remain absolutely dependent on her because he cannot yet cope with managing himself. Jimmy's sense of self is emotionally raw, and he finds it very difficult to manage separation and loss. Where he experiences times in the outside world as traumatic, the sadness that he feels is overwhelming. This brings up emotions which are a result of his early traumas and which can result in feelings of emotional abandonment from him, and ones of being attacked by others. It makes him think that he needs to control the environment that he is living in because he is afraid of losing everything he loves, but at the same time, it can result in him becoming overwhelmed with feelings of despair and sadness which can take him back to his inner feelings of emotional isolation.

Although Jimmy is now far more approachable at his times of stress than when he was originally adopted, he still requires a high degree of emotional support when he ceases to function. He does, however, have some emotional resources on which he is able to draw. Even so, there are certain circumstances in his day-to-day living when he finds the pressure of meeting the challenges which occur in certain aspects of his daily living impossible and unbearable to manage. Jimmy is functioning at the level of a fragmented/archipelago child with parts of him which have become emotionally frozen.

There are parts of the day when he is able to function well but the slightest stress factor or anxiety results in him ceasing to function. He has formed a meaningful attachment with his adoptive mother. Nevertheless, because he is so emotionally fragile and at times frozen, when under stress, he becomes in danger of disintegrating, returning to a state where his anger and overwhelming anxiety control him, affecting his behaviour.

Therapeutic Treatment Programme

Jimmy's capacity to function is limited and he can easily become overwhelmed with anxiety and fear which block his capacity to function. When he feels hopeless and helpless about his own sense of self, and despair about life, he shuts down, withdrawing into himself, and goes to his bedroom. It is important to realise this behaviour for what it represents and that because of Jimmy's early traumatic experiences, he gave up any hope of feeling positive about his own purpose in living. It was only when he was being taken care of by his older sisters and now by his adoptive mother that he feels more emotionally contained and can function. However, he is not yet ready to function positively in his own world as an individual with his own sense of purpose and individuality.

To help him move towards feeling stronger with a growing belief in his developing sense of self, the following points are important:

1 Acknowledge his feelings of anxiety and fear and let him know that you are aware and understand how painful taking risks can be for him at times. Try to help him to communicate what it is that he is afraid will happen to him, reassuring him that you will be supporting him through his painful times.
2 Help him to realise that you are aware that when he experiences situations in the outside world which makes him feel angry and sad, it can feel too much for him because perhaps it reminds him of when he felt very sad and lost as a small child. Explain that it is a very different world that he is living in now, and that you want to help him manage, and tackle the challenges he is faced with currently.

Self-esteem and self-preservation

Self-esteem

Jimmy believes that anything he attempts in life will be catastrophic, and anything good and positive could break down. He feels isolated in his day-to-day living with little or no peer support through friends. He does not yet feel ready or secure enough to integrate himself into a peer group or create friendships with others. Jimmy has little self-esteem and, at times, shows no capacity to survive his unbearable feelings. Instead, he idealises himself and sees himself as a 'hero' who is out to save the world. This represents the part of Jimmy which he feels needs protecting by his carers.

It is important to recognise that he cannot manage ambivalence and is unable to express doubts and uncertainty about his current situation and any conflicts, nor is he able to psychologically contain positive and negative feelings. Instead, he seeks situations which he can idealise, looking for a perfect solution, yet when feelings of anxiety and stress overwhelm him, he denigrates his current situation and sees his experience as being unworkable and so he tries to extinguish it, either by isolating himself or becoming aggressive and attacking others.

Self-preservation

Jimmy cannot take care of himself physically, nor can he value himself. This is most likely because he does not have any sense of enjoying and valuing any good experience he receives. Even when good experiences have occurred, they could not be perceived as a worthwhile experience for him. Jimmy's self-esteem and lack of value in himself is so intense, that he is unable to be positive about what he has experienced. In this category as before, Jimmy is a fragmented/archipelago child with bits and pieces of positive aspects of his life, but has remained frozen in his own inner world and can very easily break down and once again become negative in his reactions.

Therapeutic Treatment Programme

When Jimmy's self-esteem weakens, his sense of despair and hopelessness come to the fore, and he feels that he cannot achieve anything. His sense of self feels threatened and he attempts to destroy anything that felt positive in his life. His fear of managing reality and the challenges of the outside world are foremost in his thinking, and he ceases to try to function in external reality. This results in him falling into himself and 'hiding away' both psychologically and physically. To help his parent see him through this painful episode the following point should be thought about:

- Help Jimmy to realise that you understand that managing stress is difficult for him and give him coping mechanisms to manage them. Help him to identify what his main fears and anxieties are and how they affect him.
- Help him to identify the main areas of his day-to-day living which produces powerful emotions in him that he needs to face, identify, and focus on two areas of is day-to-day living situations, things that he needs most help with, and together write a plan as to how you can help him manage these.

- Jimmy is confused about parenting styles because he was so traumatised by his birth parents and his mind still feels that these early experiences will reoccur, even though the parenting style of his adopted parent is very different and positive. Although he desires her nurturing and responsiveness, he cannot believe that it will continue if his behaviour is difficult, and so expects hostility, emotional abandonment, and negative reactions from her. He cannot believe that a good experience will continue regardless of his behaviour.
- Jimmy requires support and help to be able to distinguish between fantasy and reality. When he is feeling emotionally fragile, his imagination takes over, and he believes that terrible things will happen and becomes the basis for his reality. He requires his mother or other carers to help him to be more realistic about his situation, which is more independent in his mind.

Help him see that reality can become more bearable and acceptable so that he can work at it with your help.

Separation and loss, managing transitions

Jimmy did not experience a good early maternal experience from which he was able to make the natural transition from absolute dependence from his mother, to a sense of inter-dependence and individuality to form the basis of his maturational development and a strengthening sense of self. In contrast, because his adoptive mother is responding to him in a very nurturing and caring manner, Jimmy feels the need to regress to an infantile stage because he finds the transition from infancy to latency and adolescence impossible to manage. Although he is now 12 years of age, there remains a part of Jimmy in his internal world which remains feeling like a two to three-year-old. It is important that both aspects are responded to by his mother without him regressing back to functioning like a two to three-year-old. Jimmy is a very vulnerable young person and this needs to be recognised.

Therapeutic Treatment Programme

The following points are important in helping Jimmy to develop greater confidence in being separated and, in beginning, to manage the process of transition:

- Help Jimmy to communicate his fears and anxieties about separating from his adopted mother. Ask him what he could take with him to help his transition to school or another change of territory. Help him to realise that you continue to hold him in your mind, thinking about him when he is not there with you.

- Try to identify what you could provide Jimmy with when he returns from school at the end of the day. By creating a space for you and him to discuss the positive and negative aspects of his day you will be providing a stepping-stone, helping him with the process of transition until he can start to think about the day himself.

Jimmy is a very emotionally fragile young person who was severely traumatised in his early years, leaving some of his emotions inside him frozen and unable to be communicated. Finding the starting point to help him manage and value himself in his new family is complicated. However, because the adoptive mother is so committed to responding and providing for his previous unmet emotional needs, there is a very strong possibility that in time she will be able to find the appropriate starting point to help him to become more emotionally integrated being able to think through his own feelings and face the reality of managing his own life.

Update on Jimmy's progress and development:

I met with Jimmy's mother two years later when he was 14 years of age. She had experienced a very difficult time with him. However, with the help and support from the post-adoption centre, and many meetings to discuss his future, he was starting to make some progress in his day-to-day living. The school he was at was not helping him at all, and he was refusing to go. He has now been placed in a 'virtual school' which specialises in educating children who are school-refusers and are unable to learn in a mainstream school. The virtual school enables him to concentrate on non-academic lessons and is focused on him learning through practical day-to-day situations. Jimmy loves working with animal care and sees that as a real opportunity for developing a career. He is also showing a great improvement in his attendance and is developing a number of functioning skills. However, Jimmy is also physically unhealthy suffering from high blood pressure and possibly diabetes. This may be partly due to the amount of anxiety and uncertainty he carries with him.

Most importantly, the foster mother has remained totally committed to helping Jimmy to feel that he exists as a person in his own right by being able to bear the unbearable thoughts and feelings he carries with him. She has always remained committed to holding Jimmy in her mind. The final result from this is that the frozen part of Jimmy is starting to unfreeze. The original Needs Led Assessment and treatment programme has helped her to deepen her own insight and understanding about Jimmy's behaviour and what it represents to both of them. There is a long way to go in her care for him, but to have found the starting point is the key to the way forward for both of them, a point that some children who have been so seriously traumatised during their early years do not achieve.

Christine Bradley
Psychotherapist

Date:

CASE STUDY OF JESSICA (*PARENTIFIED/CARETAKER*)

NLA Proforma

Identifying and understanding the trauma experienced by the child or adolescence is the first step in creating a meaningful Needs Led Assessment and Treatment Programme. This understanding helps the team to understand the symptoms of behaviour in an unintegrated child or adolescent whose maturation and developmental processes have been disrupted because of early life experiences of trauma abandonment, abuse, and deprivation.

The outcome of the assessment is to create a treatment programme, which identifies the support, communication, and provision the child or young person requires to help them to begin a process of recovery.

Needs Led Assessment and Therapeutic   **Name: JESSICA**
Treatment Programme
Name of Centre:

Name of Child: Jessica	**Date:**
Team Present: 1 Director 2 Assistant manager 3 Senior child care practitioner 4 Senior worker 5 Manager 6 Clinical psychologist 7 Christine Bradley Consultant Psychotherapist	

First Needs Assessment and Therapeutic Treatment Programme: Yes

Step 1: initial diagnosis

Currently, Jessica is 14 years of age. She has experienced and internalised a troubled and abusive early life, which was very traumatic for her. During her early years, she lived with her mother with whom she held an ambivalent relationship. Although mother's relationship with Jessica could be consistent and quite nurturing towards her, at times, she could be hostile, emotionally isolated, and aggressive towards her. Her father who has mental health problems had been quite violent towards the mother as she had often been with other men in her life. Critically, because Jessica was exposed to seeing violent behaviour towards her mother from them, she attacked her mother herself because she identified with the men's behaviour. It is also thought that Jessica may have been exposed to sexualised behaviour from the men at times. At the age of 9 years old, Jessica went to live with her aunt. Here she did experience a continuity of some good experiences and felt more emotionally contained by her, but only slightly. At the age of 12 years, she was placed in to care because of her behaviour.

Jessica is still in touch with her mother who, at times, can be consistent in her behaviour towards Jessica but not always. It is clear that Jessica is currently an emotionally fragmented child who requires a Needs Led Assessment written together with a treatment programme.

Step 2: identifying the focus of the Therapeutic Treatment Programme

The fundamental dimensions listed below are central to the child or adolescent's day-to-day living. They comprise:

1   Boundaries, merging and functioning
2   Containing emotions of anxiety, anger, and stress
3   Self-esteem and self-preservation
4   Communication
5   Learning from experience
6   Play
7   Fragile integration

As part of the discussion, the team are required to assess the level of integration and ego functioning, together with levels of non-functioning of the child or adolescent, and prioritise between two to four areas which felt are vital to their development and will form the basis of the Treatment Plan.

It was agreed to focus on the following areas:

- **Containing emotion, anxiety, anger, and stress**
- **Self-esteem and self-preservation**
- **Communication**

Treatment plan dimensions	Indicate as appropriate
Boundaries, merging and functioning	
Containing emotion, anxiety, anger, and stress	X
Self-esteem and self-preservation	X
Communication	X
Learning from experience	
Play	
Fragile Integration	

Focus of Treatment Programme

Containing emotion, anxiety, anger, and stress

Jessica cannot manage emotions. She has never been able to express her-self about her feelings which she finds unbearable to think about. Jessica continues to present as a small child who was not able to have a 'temper tantrum' nor express feelings of anger and sadness, they remain internal-ised in her emotional life at rather a primary level which makes it painful and difficult for her to manage. All her emotions of panic, rage, and un-bearable anxiety have been left inside her. Consequently, her sense of self is very fragile and she does not believe that she matters as a person in her own right.

Self-esteem and self-preservation

There is a part of Jessica which feels emotionally isolated, with her own senses and thoughts becoming too painful and unbearable to be able to think about. To survive, she has built up a 'false self'. This means that although she can exist presenting herself as charming and compliant, when she feels threatened by others, she can become overwhelmed with feelings of panic and rage which can result in her expressing a great amount of envy and rivalry towards others. Jessica's sense of self is so fragile that she finds it difficult to relate to her peers with confidence. Her low self-esteem has contributed to Jessica reaching 18 stone in weight at the height of 5'8" tall, and she is unable to value herself as a person. To survive she has become over-identified with the adult aggression and abuse experienced in her early life which gave her no space to feel comfortable with herself as a small child. The small child remains locked inside her, unable to strengthen and grow emotionally. She has identified with the adults who could not emotionally contain and nurture her with a sense of safety and security. Physically, Jessica presents no pride about herself at all. She desires to be liked by her peers and to become a part of group activities, but because she is deeply emotionally fragile and feels negatively about her own appearance, she can create situations where others become negative towards her. As a consequence, she remains somewhat of a recluse.

In light of these observations, it is becoming clear that Jessica is presenting as a 'False self', having become a 'Parentified/Caretaker' Child to survive.

Communication

Jessica is not able to communicate through words about her feelings. However, through the use of symbolic communication, she can start to express some of her fears and uncertainties. She needs more opportunities for art and finding ways of expressing herself through more creative outlets.

Step 3: Therapeutic Treatment Programme

The Needs Led Assessment Programme has identified that Jessica is functioning at the level of a parentified/caretaker child who has developed a 'false self' in order to survive.

A false self, when under pressure, experiences anxiety that can becomes unthinkable and often leads to unpredictable outbursts. In order to survive the degree of anxiety and uncertainty that she feels because of the lost child inside her, she has built up a way of surviving that does not relate to the real Jessica, who remains deeply uncertain about herself and life.

Treatment programme

- Holding in mind. Jessica needs to be aware that her workers are thinking about her in a sense which feels real to her. If she isolates herself, ask her why is it that she would rather be on her own. Remember there is a very lost child in her who has always felt on her own. Let her know that you are aware of her need to protect herself. Ask her what is it she is afraid of when she is having to face the realities of the outside world.

- Think of the element of primary provision which she requires if she is to feel the little self is being recognised then she can hand the little self over to the worker and can start to think about the other part of Jessica that is afraid of the outside world. I will think with you about the provision of primary experiences for unintegrated children and young people.
- Give her as many opportunities to play as is appropriate for her.
- Parentified/caretaker children often communicate at a symbolic level so it could be through her artistic and creative side that she will be able to communicate symbolically. It is important that workers do not react negatively to what she is communicating symbolically, so a more an interested response from them will help her to feel that she is being held in the mind of the worker and recognised positively by them.

Remember that it is important to realise that the 'parentified/caretaker self' looks after their own little self who remains locked inside to protect themselves from the outside world.

Conclusion

It is clear that Jessica has developed a parentified/caretaker self to survive some of the unbearable experiences that she was subjected to as a child. The Therapeutic Treatment Programme should enable the team to provide her with the help so that she can gain a stronger sense of self about her identity.

Follow-up Needs Led Assessment: date for next meeting

A future meeting for a follow-up assessment and treatment programme has been arranged to take place in three months' time.

Christine Bradley
Psychotherapist

Date:

Update on Jessica's progress and development:

The Needs Led Assessment and Therapeutic Treatment Programme identified Jessica as being non-functioning at a very deep level. This is because the emotions and feelings of panic and rage, which she experienced as a small child, remain trapped inside her. These can be acted out at a very primitive level when she is faced with stress factors in her day-to-day living which she has to face. It can result in her acting out her powerful emotions which she cannot afford to think about, through violence or destructive behaviour at a primitive level. The assessment tells us that Jessica's experiences of her mother were often centred through violent behaviour towards herself and at times others. Such pathological defences in Jessica can often lead to her becoming violent towards those responsible for her. Because she became 'frozen' with her emotions, she was not able to make meaningful relationships with others or express real concern towards them.

Sadly, when I enquired about the outcome for Jessica, I was informed that because of her violent behaviour towards the adults in the team and to other children and young people, the team did not feel that they could contain her safely, and the placement broke down. Further, this resulted in other homes not being able to contain her either when her violent episodes took over. This was her only sense of a personal identity which was constantly being acted out against others because of her early trauma of violence and abuse. Jessica is a 'Frozen child' whose mind is not able to think about her behaviour.

It may have helped the team if they had the opportunity to reflect on the following key areas when thinking about the assessment and treatment programmes for Jessica:

- The use of reflective logs in their work.
- A deeper understanding about the concept of transference and counter-transference between themselves and the children and young people they are responsible for.
- Working with separation and loss as key factors for unintegrated children and young people.
- Understanding the concepts of verbal, non-verbal, and symbolic communication in therapeutic work with children and young people.
- The lesson to be learnt by us all, in this case, is that the concept of the frozen child is a truly complex one which needs understanding at a deep level by those working with them.

CASE STUDY: KEIRA *(FRAGMENTED/ARCHIPELAGO CHILD WITH A 'FROZEN' SENSE OF SELF)*

First Need Led Assessment and Therapeutic Treatment Programme: Yes

Date:

Background

Kiera is 14 years of age. Her early childhood experiences have been turbulent and traumatic for lengthy periods and her family experiences have involved serious criminal activity, drug use, and domestic violence. Her relationship with her mother was very ambivalent and without any meaningful relationship developing between them both, she also experienced considerable tension and conflict between her mother and paternal grandparents. This left her feeling emotionally abused by her parents and she was given no positive boundaries which could help her to feel emotionally contained.

Keira did have a younger brother who was two years younger than her, and with whom she has good memories, but he was also removed from the family home. As a result of the traumatic and abusive experiences Keira went through at home, she was left feeling emotionally very fragile with her sense of self becoming deeply vulnerable with no sense of belonging nor a safe place to be herself. Consequently, in her early adolescence, it is thought that she became a victim of sexual exploitation. Consequently, her behaviour at school became more and more difficult and disruptive, eventually she was excluded. She was also removed from the home situation and placed into two foster home settings, both of which broke down, because of her destructive and self-destructive behaviour being acted out in the placements. Although Keira has received some help from CAMHs teams, there is no sign of her behaviour and feelings about herself improving. She remains a fragmented, unintegrated child with little or no sense of self starting to grow and develop.

Keira was placed in a residential children's Home at the age of ten. Her behaviour since that time has created much concern and anxiety in the staff team. To help them develop a deeper insight and understanding about her behaviour, it has been agreed that a Needs Led Assessment will be discussed and written, together with a therapeutic treatment programme designed to understand and meet her needs at both a primary and secondary level. The aim is to help Keira to reach a stage of emotional integration, more able to learn from her experiences and develop meaningful relationships of dependency and attachment with those who are responsible for her.

A Need Led Assessment Programme focuses on the child or young person's day-to-day living experiences identifying how they can or cannot manage them. It is designed to help workers to identify the children's emotional needs which require support and provision after the assessment has been completed and a therapeutic treatment plan put together.

Focus of Therapeutic Treatment Programme

It was agreed that the two therapeutic treatment programme dimensions that would provide the focus for meeting Kiera's needs were:

- **Boundaries, merging and functioning**
- **Self-destruction and self-preservation**

Boundaries, merging and functioning

Keira cannot hold onto boundaries and follow rules, since the presentation of reality is too frightening for her and can often result in her becoming destructive or self-destructive in her behaviour. As she did not experience a relationship of absolute dependency in her early days with her mother, she continues to seek a merger with others, this can often lead her into relationships where she feels attacked by them as she seeks out the anti-social tendency, becoming overwhelmed by panic, rage, and unthinkable anxiety. Alternatively, she can resist interacting with others and retreat into her own inner world where she feels isolated and emotionally abandoned. Keira avoids male attention but seeks relationships with females. However, although she seeks female attention, she is also afraid of making meaningful contact with them and is resistant to forming a relationship which becomes significant and important to her because her early infantile relationships have been driven by conflict, tension, and abandonment. As a result, she holds many fears and anxieties about managing the reality of her day-to-day living because she believes that the painful and traumatic experiences she went through previously, will reoccur again from the female workers at the Home. This is because Keira's sense of self is very fragile and vulnerable. She cannot manage boundaries on her own and finds the realities of the external world difficult and quite unbearable to manage. Keira's internal working model does not align with the external realities she has to face.

Although there are parts of her day-to-day living when she can function, the slightest stress factor can prevent her from functioning as she becomes either destructive, disrupting others preventing them from functioning, or self-destructive, harming herself and cutting off from the outside world.

Here, Keira was assessed as a fragmented/archipelago child with limited areas of functioning with parts of her which have become emotionally frozen.

Therapeutic Treatment Programme

When Keira's behaviour is becoming aggressive and destructive, it is important not to react to her as she will experience that as an attack on her own self physically and emotionally, and respond by becoming more attacking on others. Respond to her, letting her know that you are experiencing her behaviour as a sign that she is feeling frightened and overwhelmed by others. Ask whether there anything you can do to help her to feel better about how she is feeling.

Because she finds being part of a group difficult to manage, let her know that you will be with her when appropriate. If it is not possible to be with her, let her know that you will be thinking about her. Keira needs to be aware that you are constantly holding her in your mind.

Be careful not to idealise her when she functions, she may find the expectations that she continues to function well, too difficult to achieve, which could result in Keira 'acting out', because of her anxieties. When she ceases to function in any day-to-day situation, it is important not to express your disappointment to her. When her functioning diminishes that could be the time when she requires some structured primary provision from you.

Self-destruction and self-preservation

Keira's sense of self is so fragile that she cannot respond to other people's emotions. She has little or no belief in herself as an individual in her own right. Rather, she has spent her life surviving unbearable fears and anxieties about life and living. The slightest stress results in her breaking down and acting out destructively and self-destructively. When being destructive to others, she has been known to lash out, damage property and assault her peers, and has also attempted to assault members of the staff team at the Home. Regarding Her self-destructive behaviour, she has been known to burn herself with cigarettes, and cut herself. Keira has little or no self-esteem. There is an emotionally-trapped child in Keira's inner world, who feels lost and abandoned but who often emerges when under stress to expresses herself.

Because Kiera has learnt to survive her life experiences and traumas, rather than learn how to live with them, and although she can take care of herself, and keeps herself tidy, she is not able to keep up with the rules of others. Pressure from the outside world can result in the acting out her destructive and self-destructive emotions. Her expectation of reality is that there will be violence and so she survives, accordingly. Keira has built a 'false self' in herself in order to survive unbearable anxieties and fears, which can only result in breakdown at times of stress.

Here, Keira functions as a fragmented/archipelago child with levels of her sense of being, which are 'frozen'.

Addressing Kiera's self-esteem

Advice to Team:

Because Kiera's self- esteem is so low, she places little value on herself and finds it very difficult to think about her emotions. Consequently, too much reaction from her workers can recreate the emotions of panic and rage, which have become frozen in her inner world which when it explodes can be acted out destructively or self-destructively. Remember if she arouses strong feelings in you as the carer or worker, it is important that you can **respond** to her actions rather than **react** to them. It is all too easy for Keira to project her own anxieties onto the worker and without professional support for the carer or worker for them to transfer their own negative transference feelings back onto Keira.

Addressing emotions of hopelessness and helplessness

Advice to Team:

Kiera needs constant encouragement from you, she believes that any positive experience will not continue and so will try to prevent it from continuing, thus bringing out the negativity in her and emotions of hopelessness and helplessness.

Helping Kiera manage her anxiety

Advice to Team:

Put some thought into understanding what creates anxiety in Keira, and learn to respond accordingly. When her anxiety reaches extremes, her sense of self will feel threatened. Suggest that perhaps you find a quiet space where you can sit down with a drink or special food and think about what is making her feel so terrible, and together you can think about a way which could help her to feel better. This could help some of her most unbearable emotions to unfreeze and use the provision that you are offering to her.

Meeting of Primary and Secondary Needs

Advice to Team:

The meeting of primary needs represents the maternal and primary provision given to an infant in the early years of their development. If they have been traumatised in their early years it leaves them feeling emotionally fragile and vulnerable with their mentalisation process remaining at a very early stage of development, and stuck in the areas of lost or absent early experiences. The statement describes the difficulties Keira has been overwhelmed with in her day-to-day living circumstances. The therapeutic task is for her workers to provide a good experience for her, which she did not feel emotionally provided for in her early years through feeding, holding, and feeling emotionally contained by those responsible for her. It is important that workers decide the appropriate provision for her, which will be provided for her by those she could become dependent on, and that it continues to be provided for her until she no longer requires it. What provision will need to be discussed and arranged during the treatment plan meeting. As Keira begins to feel more nurtured, emotionally, and physically contained by her workers, she will begin to move forward towards emotional integration.

The meeting of Keira's secondary needs represents supporting her to build up her emotional resources as she starts to believe in herself, her levels of ego functioning will increase and strengthen, but she will require some considerable support from her workers to help her to continue developing.

Hopelessness and helplessness

Advice to Team:

As Keira's sense of self is very low and fragile, she finds it very difficult to give up on feeling negative about herself. To help Keira move on from her own sense of despair and feelings of hopelessness and helplessness, which can result in her emotions of panic, rage, and unthinkable anxiety being acted out. As she begins to depend on what you are providing for her, by continuing to respond to her unbearable emotions and understand how unbearable it can feel for her at times, she could begin to express herself in a more meaningful way. As she begins to feel that what remained impossible for her to achieve, life could slowly begin to feel more possible for her. This could present her with a stronger sense of hope about her emotional development and finding the ability to manage the outside world positively and creatively. It could give her a stronger way forward in her own development.

False self and real self

Advice to Team:

To receive therapeutic treatment at the Home, it is important that workers do not collude with the false self because:

> The false self is built up on a basis of compliance. It can have a defensive function which is the protection of the true self. Only the true self can feel real, but the true self must never be affected by external reality, and must never comply. When the false self becomes exploited and treated as real there is a growing sense in the individual of futility and despair.
>
> (Winnicott 1965:132)

If Keira is to be prevented from being overwhelmed by her hopelessness and helplessness, it is important that workers do not collude with her false self which leaves her in danger of her fantasy about the outside world becoming a reality.

Conclusion:

Keira is a very complex child, who currently remains at a level of unintegration with little or no sense of self, and not yet ready to make an attachment relationship. Before she can reach that stage, she requires a stage of becoming absolutely dependent on her workers, with a continuity of good experiences from them. The use of the therapeutic treatment programme over the following months should help her to move towards a stage of fragile integration, i.e., developing a sense of self, beginning to make attachment relationships in the home. Taking her to this stage could be a difficult and painful time in part for the carers and workers responsible for her, as they begin to get in touch with her inner world sense of abandonment, but the outcome should be more rewarding to both Keira and the team.

Christine Bradley
Psychotherapist

Date:

Update on Keira's progress and development:

After a two-year break, I approached the team to discuss Keira's progress and development, following on from their use of the Needs Led Assessment and Therapeutic Treatment Programmes. I was informed that sadly her placement with the Home had to be terminated because of the constant level of aggression towards the team and others which was at times quite violent.

Keira had also become very involved with a high level of sub-cultural delinquent activities with a group of adolescents and young people near the Home which had led into more and more trouble with the police. Critically, Keira had internalised her mother's violent and aggressive behaviour so it had become part of her personal identity which made it very difficult for her to function positively without breaking down and acting out destructively towards others. Additionally, she merged with others identifying with other people's (men) violence and could not be contained from over-identifying with them, which resulted in her acting out their aggressive behaviour. This defence mechanism of a victim identifying with the aggressor in order to survive, meant that Keira took on the role of the aggressor.

Conclusions

The case studies presented in this chapter illustrate the use of Needs Led Assessments followed by Therapeutic Treatment Programmes. They have been put together to help the team of therapeutic workers and carers to identify the necessary skills and understanding that enable them to respond with a deeper insight enabling them to meet the emotional needs of those for whom they are responsible, with greater confidence. The case studies have illustrated that it is not easy task to help children and young people who had been deeply traumatised in their early years to begin to feel better about themselves and to begin the process of developing a sense of their own self which they can learn to live with positively and thoughtfully. Being able to examine the long-term outcomes for these young people and question whether the assessment and treatment programme requires more thought can help us to make the necessary changes to the treatment and practice to help support and strengthen maturational development. The inclusion of the reflective log written by the team of workers and carers about their therapeutic practise with the children and young people is an important addition since it helps to deepen their understanding and insight about reaching 'the heart of the matter' in what is very complex work. The new model of case studies, which includes the use of reflective logs highlights that using these, has helped the teams to deliver a better outcome for the children and young people for whom they are responsible.

Christine Bradley
Psychotherapist

Date:

Chapter 5

Long-term prognosis of traumatised children into adolescence and adulthood

Christine Bradley and Francia Kinchington

The impact of traumatic experiences on infants and young children in their early childhood

For over a hundred years, we have worked on understanding early trauma and the negative impact that it has on the emotional development of infants and young children, and it is as relevant today as it has been historically. The insight into early trauma, its impact, and treatment has been addressed by two pioneers in the field John Bowlby and Donald Winnicott, who have laid the foundations of our work today. However, we also need to recognise that within the past 30 years a deeper understanding about how neuroscience and clinical psychology have contributed to the framework of thinking about the management of traumatic experiences in young children and how we can help them to survive what they have been exposed to. These overwhelming and unbearable experiences have been shown to make changes in the brain through the release of cortisol during stress, arresting the normal processes of emotional and cognitive brain development.

Dr. John Bowlby dedicated his working life to researching, understanding, and investigating the concept of attachment theory, to identify how the deprivation and privation of negative emotional experiences and physical abuse in their early years could produce negative and far-reaching consequences for young children. He showed that the infant was unable to develop emotionally, at a time when the maturational processes were working towards the development of their sense of self and becoming an individual in their own right.

Dr. Donald Winnicott focused on the development of the self and emotional development in young children and the impact that early deprivation and ongoing abusive experiences that the child was exposed to in their early life and the negative affect had on their capacity to function positively in their later life. Donald Winnicott in researching and understanding the development of the self in children and young people has made a significant impact on the work in the field by addressing the importance of creative thinking in helping workers to present well-thought-through therapeutic practise when they are working with children who have been deeply traumatised in their early years.

DOI: 10.4324/9781032657592-5

In my early years of therapeutic practise, I was influenced by Winnicott's thinking when he was involved with helping myself and others to think about what it means to us when we are responsible for children and adolescents who had been deeply traumatised in their early life and how it has prevented them from being able to manage the outside world. Significantly, Bowlby towards the end of his life declared "I always held the view that Winnicott and I were singing the same tune. We were essentially giving the same message, but again he didn't like my theoretical ideas" (Bradley and Kinchington, 2018: 62).

The following section draws on the work of Bowlby and Winnicott.

Bowlby defined attachment theory as providing a secure base and a grounding point for emotional development from where attachment relationships could begin. Attachment disorders arise where the secure base breaks down as a result of trauma and results in the following behaviours which can prevent healthy and secure attachment relationships from developing:

- Avoidant/resistant/helpless/hostile
- Disorganised and controlling
- Dysregulated
- Avoidant/ambivalent/resistant/dependent

Pre-attachment relates to the first three months of life during which period the secure base is formed through the mother-infant bonding so that the infant feels emotionally contained, and bonded with her. Where bonding does not take place within the first six months, it impacts in a profound way on the emotional maturation of healthy infant growth and development. It limits the infant's ability to fulfil their potential and can, at times, cause them to regress to infantile states of despair and panic.

Winnicott described emotional integration as feeling whole and complete as a person with a sense of self, exhibiting empathy and remorse and the capacity to evolve defence mechanisms that protect the self and valuing meaningful relationships in which they can share the world with others.

Unintegration

The unintegrated child has little or no sense of self and feels emotionally isolated or seeks to merge with others. The child does not feel held in mind or emotionally contained by their primary carers and has no sense of absolute dependence on them, holding a fear of emotional and physical abandonment which is more powerful than a sense of secure emotional holding.

Anxieties are more primitive, with no boundaries between fantasy and reality in their day-to-day living. It leaves the child unable to learn from their experiences and with a tendency to recreate destructive or self-destructive behaviour when they are overwhelmed with panic, rage, and unthinkable anxiety.

How can we recognise the complex and difficult behaviour presented by a child as representing their anxieties and fears which have emerged because of their traumatic experiences and respond to them accordingly? Winnicott described the unintegrated child as one who was not able to develop a strong sense of self from which they could find out about, and question the outside world and how it functioned. Rather, the child viewed the outside world as a place outside their inner world as hostile, and which could become attacking and destructive towards them so they felt compelled to attack them back.

He described four levels of un-integration and the work which was required to enable children and young people to recover from their early trauma and move towards functioning without breaking down. These are the frozen child, the archipelago (now described as fragmented) child and the caretaker (now described as parentified child), and fragile integration.

The frozen child

The trauma of the frozen child relates to the earliest parts of the infant's existence when their experiences were so full of emotional abandonment, lacking a personal sense of feeling emotionally held onto by their primary carer, and without any sense of receiving containment or ongoing nurturing. The infant and the child they later become, have no sense of belonging or relationship with their primary carer, and the centre of their inner world becomes frozen. If their experiences are compounded by further emotional trauma, their inner world continues to remain 'frozen'. They begin to function at a superficial level only and can very easily break down into acting out. This can lead to destructive and self-destructive outcomes in their life. Appropriate responsive support and care by carers and workers working therapeutically can help the frozen parts of the child begin to 'unfreeze'.

The following understanding of integration and unintegration needs to be considered.

- The frozen child is unable to manage the intimacy of attachment relationships. Carers and workers need to adapt to meeting their dependency needs in small ways that do not threaten them.
- The child needs to be constantly held in mind by their workers and carers who are responsible for them because they did not experience this with their primary carer.
- The child disrupts boundaries and develops their own reality which for them is safer, than living with actual reality.
- The child has very few areas of functioning in their day-to-day living. These mask panic and rage which can be acted out destructively and self-destructively under the slightest stress.

The archipelago (fragmented) child

This term describes a child who was exposed to traumatic experiences in their early years, and although they did have short periods of good enough care and provision from their primary carer and felt held in their mind by them, this did not continue. Unfortunately, their good experience with their carers broke down, for whatever reason, before the infant was ready to make the transition to become more interdependent from their carer, working with their own sense of self as a separate person in their own right. Although they had made their first step towards emotional integration, they were unable to continue developing through the maturational process, leaving them with a sense of self that was raw and fragile, leaving them vulnerable to breaking down, and at times, ceasing to function. However, because of the brief good experiences they did receive, they have the potential inner resources to rebuild their life with appropriate help and support from their carers to build appropriate defence mechanisms rather than 'survival' techniques which can become destructive and anti-social for them.

The caretaker child (parentified)

The caretaker (parentified) child represents the child who in their early years received good experiences from a carer with whom they felt emotionally contained and secure. The carer might not have been the mother, but perhaps a foster carer, or a kinship carer for a period in either a family or specialist residential setting. During their time with the carer, the infant will have felt 'held in mind' by them, which was very important in helping them to develop a secure sense of self. Unfortunately, this experience did not continue for any length of time because the placement was forced to end after a short period before they were able to manage and resolve their transition from dependence to interdependence. Critically, they experienced a sense of loss before they were ready to let go of their sense of absolute dependence with their carer. As a result, the infant is left with a sense of loss and the need to substitute an 'alternative' mother by becoming their own carer. This early loss could impede the positive developmental growth and transition into the next stage of their life because they remained in a state of over-identification with their alternative carer on whom they were dependent and unable to separate and make a transition into independence. They present themselves as the caretaker based on the early experience of their original carer but the little self remains locked inside them, left abandoned by the adults who were caring for them.

The following guidance is aimed at helping the child or young person to reach a level of emotional independence by enabling the care or worker to help the child to reach through to the trapped lost child that is preventing their emotional development. The following will help therapeutic carers and workers to respond to the child or young person with meaning, enabling the slow process of development to take place.

The caretaker (parentified) child needs support to hand the 'caretaker self' over to the worker or carer. This should be done through a process of negotiation which allows the 'caretaker self' to feel in control of the 'little self' in their day-to-day living. These children find transitions difficult to manage. The child needs support for their confidence, which can be fragile at times, particularly when they are dealing with separation and loss in their day-to-day living.

Whilst the caretaker (parentified) child finds stress difficult to manage, they are more likely to have temper tantrums rather than 'acting out' their panic and rage which they cannot communicate about because they did have the foundation of some positive maternal experiences in their early life. They are nearer the point of integration being able to put their feelings and thinking together, but they will require a great amount of support and help if they are to move forward to the next stage of maturation and emotional development of their sense of self.

It is important to recognise that the caretaker (parentified) child is located at a stage that is slightly behind the child who has reached a stage of fragile integration. It signifies a situation where even though the infant or small child did make an initial relationship with the primary carer, the attachment did not form a secure enough base to enable a secure or dependable way of enabling the child to manage the needs of their inner world and the demands of the external world. Consequently, there are times when their sense of self can be vulnerable, and their emotional fragility and lack of organisation make them unable to resolve painful issues in their day-to-day lives. Importantly, in both cases, of the caretaker (parentified) and fragile integration, a number good experiences have occurred where the child felt held in mind by their carers, and so although feeling emotionally fragile at times, with therapeutic support they can manage to find their way through times of stress because the child has a developing sense of self.

Fragile integration

In contrast to the earlier stages, fragile integration denotes an insecure attachment but one where that the child has the beginnings of a sense of self even though still vulnerable. Although they are beginning to come together as a person, they still feel very fragile and can easily break down when confronted with stressful situations. Even though this sense of self is not yet strong enough, nevertheless it is sufficient to enable the child or young person to manage stressful factors in their life. Reality is still very difficult to manage and needs emotional support if they are not to break down. The child shows evidence of beginning to make transitions, from being absolutely dependent to becoming relatively dependent on others, as when the individual starts to relate to others outside the nurturing of the primary carer. It is important to recognise that without support from their carers, they can remain emotionally stuck in their maturational development.

This section of the chapter has outlined the importance of carers and workers deepening their insight and understanding about the impact of traumatic episodes in the early lives of children and young people, helping them to identify how they can support their recovery through the use of therapeutic care, Needs Led Assessment, and individualised therapeutic treatment programmes.

The legacy of trauma into adulthood

The second part of this chapter explores the impact of profound trauma experienced in infancy and early childhood. Without a doubt, the repercussions are far-reaching, extending into adolescence, adulthood, and old age. Although some children and young people experience the advantage and support of kinship care, good foster care, or adoption, for others, their lives are characterised by childhoods spent in short- and long-term foster care and residential children's homes, often lacking consistent long-term care, and experiencing fractured relationships. These experiences impact not only on the young person but also on the adult they become. These early experiences impact on self-identity and confidence, their health and wellbeing, their capacity to learn and engage in education, mental health, interpersonal and social relationships; their relationship with food, alcohol, and drugs; their sense of safety and trust; and extends into their relationships with partners, friends, and their own children. These experiences create the lens through which they see the world around them, creating an underlying and pervasive sense of anxiety and insecurity.

The pattern of transitions, which are normally experienced by young people who have the advantage of secure attachments and safe and stable family relationships, is a given, signalling the changes from dependence to independence, from childhood to adolescence and adulthood. They include moving from primary to secondary school, leaving school, going into further and higher education, getting a job, developing mature relations and independent living and adulthood, and evolving a safety net of family and friendships.

In contrast, the care leaver is faced with major issues on leaving the social care system at the age of 17 or 18. Ensuring secure living arrangements, managing financially, concerns about trust and safety, finding a job, continuing education, managing latent mental health issues, health, sexual, and dental care, and even shopping and cooking are real issues and sources of anxiety. Feelings of isolation, having to move away from a community or area with which they are familiar and being cut off from existing networks, having to develop new friendships and relationships, and concerns for their future are sources of real anxiety, which they are often left to navigate on their own without appropriate safety-net provision.

In addition, it is important to recognise that a young person's vulnerabilities, for example, in terms of needing to be 'held in mind', transference/projection of their emotions on others, their capacity to accept personal responsibility for their actions, the defence mechanisms that the deploy to manage the outer world, their ability to contain emotion, anger and stress, their propensity for self-destruction, and their ability to handle transitions, do not disappear when the young person leaves the care system and forced into independent living at the age of 18.

Five specific areas have been singled out for closer examination, providing a glimpse of life for the young person having to manage living 'outside'.

 i Transition from care to independent living
 ii Learning and education
iii Mental health
iv Interpersonal and social relationships
 v Youth offending and custody

Transition from care to independent living

It is a real concern that young people who leave the case system either through foster care or residential home arrangements (financial and statutory) find themselves ill-prepared for independent living. Although statutory guidance requires that young people should be introduced to their personal adviser (PA) from age 16, over a quarter of care leavers did not meet their PA until they were 18 or older, and some about to leave care still did not know who would be helping them (Ofsted, 2022b). Housing, personal safety, caring for themselves, managing money, and basic skills such as shopping and cooking are real issues. Many care leavers reported that they were not taught essential skills, such as how to shop, cook, the process of paying bills, and managing money. The report on care leavers preparing to leave care identified that more than a third of care leavers felt that they left care too early. Of those who did feel that they left care at the right time, not all felt they had the required skills to live more independently. Critically, many care leavers were not prepared for the accommodation or location they ended up living in. Some were living alone for the first time, living with strangers, or living in an area they did not know or did not feel safe in. Sometimes, fears about living alone or in unfamiliar or unsafe areas led to young people feeling pressured to make decisions that they did not want to make, including reconnecting with family members who may have been a risk to them, moving in with abusive partners, or engaging in criminal activity to gain money.

Finding safe, stable accommodation in an area that the young person is familiar with is a real issue on leaving care. MacAlister (2022: 214) reported that young people who had come from a care background often found themselves forced into poor quality or unstable accommodation with little support after leaving care at a young age. The recommendation of his report was that young people should feel able to push for better accommodation without fear of falling foul of 'homelessness intentionality' rules where they made themselves deliberately homeless since the local authority has a role as a 'corporate parent' and would still be obliged to provide, often more costly, services as a consequence.

Learning and education

The potential of a positive school experience and its capacity to turn young lives around cannot be underestimated. Van der Kolk (2014: 422) observes that

> *The greatest hope for traumatized, abused, and neglected children is to receive a good education in schools where they are seen and known, where they learn to regulate themselves, and where they can develop a sense of agency. At their best, schools can function as islands of safety in a chaotic world. They can teach children how their bodies and brains work and how they can understand and deal with their emotions.*

Developing a positive learner identity lays down the roots for formal education, self-education and development, a willingness to return to education as an adult, the capacity to reflect on and learn from experience, and the development of practical and problem-solving skills into adult help. A positive learner identity offers adults the potential to make changes in one's life, to learn from both negative and positive experiences, to learn from others, and to take responsibility for one's behaviour and actions.

A failure of the school system to meet the child's learning needs, whether arising from disrupted education, or undiagnosed dyslexia or ADHD, will have a profound impact on the adult's self-esteem and identity and inevitably limit access to jobs that involve learning and qualifications. The Ministry of Justice statistics (2021) reported that 57% of adult prisoners taking initial assessments had literacy levels below those expected of 11-year-olds. The educational progression of this group of young people into further or higher education is poor (DfE, 2015: 13), showing that at the age of 17, only 49% were in some form of education (34% were in education, 15% in training or employment), with 27% not in employment, education or training (NEET), and 24%, for whom no information was known. For 18-year-olds, 46% were known to be in education, 18% were in training or employment but concerningly, 30% were NEET, and additional 6% for whom no information was known. Poor education and qualifications restrict the opportunities available to adults and without focused government and social interventions such as apprenticeship schemes, work experience and training schemes, opportunities for work, and the potential they bring are severely restricted.

On a positive note, Sacker et al. (2021: 46) in the Looked-after Children Grown-up project (LACGro) identified that the predicted rates of employment in the 20s were particularly low for those who had been in care; however, there appeared to be return to education in their 30s and by their 40s, so that these adults were predicted to have only a slightly lower rate of employment than those who had only been in parental care. Additionally, they noted upward social mobility and improved housing tenure.

Mental and physical health

The developmental and mental health problems reported for children and young people who had experienced trauma have been associated with adolescent engagement in delinquent and violent activities, risky sexual behaviours, and suicidal/self-mutilating behaviours (Leslie et al., 2005) and increased rates of post-traumatic stress, depression and anxiety, antisocial behaviours, and greater risk for alcohol and substance use disorders in adolescence and adulthood (De Bellis and Zisk, 2014). Negele et al. (2015) identified emotional abuse, sexual abuse, and critically, multiple exposures to childhood trauma in a high number of chronically depressed adult patients.

It was found that adults who spent time in care between 1971 and 2001 were 70% more likely to die prematurely than those who did not, and also more likely to experience an unnatural death (defined as self-harm, accidents, and mental and behavioural causes) (Murray et al., 2020).

Sacker et al. (2021: 32) analysed data on the health of adults who had care experiences when young and found an association between residential care, as compared to other forms of care, and limiting long-term illness. Although it was considered that this was potentially in part due to pre-existing health conditions which resulted in children being placed in residential care rather than kinship or foster care, further detailed analysis showed that the risk between limiting long-term illness and residential care still stood at the 30-year follow-up.

Interpersonal and social relationships

The experience of profound trauma experienced by infants and young children increases the prospect of maladaptive defence mechanisms developed in early childhood which enable the child to live with and manage the extreme emotional anxiety and external stressors experienced in their day-to-day life, continuing into adolescence and adulthood. The resulting learnt behaviours nevertheless persist and may become modified in adulthood and even masked, providing an emotional support that enables the individual to manage their life. The following exemplifies the defence strategies used by adults to manage the legacy of early trauma, their relationships, and the complexity of adult life:

- **Acting out** by expressing feelings or impulses towards partners and significant others in response to interpersonal events in the form of uncontrolled behaviour disregarding the personal or social consequences.
- **Altruism** is enacted to help to gratify social and attachment needs whilst dealing with emotional conflict such as powerless and anger, to make up for past experiences where help was needed but unavailable through helping others.
- **Autistic fantasy** involves relying on excessive daydreaming as a substitute for human relationships, action, or trying to solve the problems that they are faced with.
- **Denial** is used to avoid dealing with a situation that the individual finds stressful, but only ends up creating a disconnect between them and reality.
- **Passive aggression** by indirectly and unassertively expressing aggression towards others where the intensity of the aggression that they feel is masked by the way it is expressed.
- **Projection** where unacknowledged feelings, impulses, or thoughts are falsely attributing to someone else, either someone who they feel threatened by such as someone they work with, or have some kind of feeling towards.
- **Rationalisation** involves creating reassuring or plausible justifications explaining away events, their own behaviour, or that of others which hide the individual's underlying thoughts, feeling, or motivations.
- **Repression** is the unconscious blocking of difficult or traumatic experiences from one's conscious thinking protecting the individual from being consciously aware of what had been experienced in the past.

- **Suppression** involves temporarily postponing avoiding thinking about disturbing problems, wishes, feelings, or experiences.
- **Intellectualisation** enables the individual to distance themselves from uncomfortable experiences or unpleasant emotions, impulses, or behaviours by using facts, logic, and intellectual reasoning to avoid having to deal with the emotional aspects of the experiences.

Youth offending and custody

Williams et al. (2012) examined the childhood, family circumstances, and patterns of reoffending of 1,435 prisoners who had been newly sentenced in 2005 and 2006, and reported that:

> *Twenty-four per cent stated that they had been in care at some point during their childhood. Those who had been in care were younger when they were first arrested, and were more likely to be reconvicted in the year after release from custody than those who had never been in care. Many prisoners had experienced abuse (29%) or observed violence in the home (41%) as a child – particularly those who stated that they had a family member with an alcohol or drug problem. Those who reported experiencing abuse or observing violence as a child were more likely to be reconvicted in the year after release than those who did not. (ii)*

Fitzpatrick et al. (2016: 8) report that the offending rates of children in care are around four times higher than those of all other children, with 5.6% of looked after children aged 10 – 17 receiving a conviction, final warning or reprimand during the year ending 31 March 2014. A third of young males in prison custody had previously been in care, as had 9 out of 16 girls, highlighting the even greater over-representation of females. The complexity of their backgrounds shows that they are more likely to be exposed to the risk factors relating to deprivation, poor parenting, abuse, and neglect which contributed to a range of emotional, social, and behavioural difficulties, including anti-social and offending behaviour. MacAlister (2022: 164) reported that currently Young Offender Institutions (YOIs) and Secure Training Centres (STCs) are wholly unsuitable for children in that they are unable to break the cycle of offending or offer training. The key question to be asked is, given their history, whether incarceration is the most appropriate action in the case of this group of adolescents in an effort to change behaviours and prevent a cycle of recidivism in adulthood.

Looking to the future

Although some adults who carry the legacy and wounds of profound trauma live limited lives, others are able to channel their anger, the injustice of what they experienced, and their creativity into productive lives where they are recognised and celebrated as individuals, not as victims. The walls of the Foundling Museum in London list the names of over 100 characters from literature whose stories are familiar and inspire both children and adults, and which as an institution is supported by the Foundling Fellows, who represent all fields of the arts. People in everyday life overcome their early experiences to become inspirational teachers in schools and universities, in health and social care, in the police and armed forces, become nurses and doctors, work in the building trade, are actors, musicians, poets, counsellors, and business people, and importantly have loving families of their own. They are able to recognise the role played by key people in their lives who saw beyond the shattered children that they were and gave them the possibility of hope for their future and showed them that lives could be turned around. The role of good kinship care and therapeutic care cannot be underestimated.

Chapter 6

Supporting and developing carers and workers

Francia Kinchington

This chapter examines the critical role of carers and workers in creating therapeutic environments in which they can function emotionally and professionally to support children and young people who live with the legacy of profound trauma.

The setting itself is an important distinction in terms of the support available to the carers and workers. Either the individual responsible cares or works exclusively with a child in their home, or they work as part of a team in a school or care setting. These range from an individual setting as in the case of a foster carer, or adoptive parent, to a group setting as in the case of a worker in a residential children's home, therapeutic or otherwise, a secure unit or part of a team working with unaccompanied minors. The other group who will have direct responsibility for children who have been identified as being at risk by social services are schools (whether mainstream, special, virtual, or pupil referral units), their headteachers, and special needs teachers who are likely to be responsible for the children's day-to-day education. The distinction between an individual or group setting is important in terms of the daily support available to them in carrying out their role. Carers in an individual setting essentially work with the children and young people for whom they are responsible on their own with access to other professionals as the need arises.

In contrast, carers and workers who are part of a group setting, as in a residential children's home, work as part of a team where they have daily access to colleagues and managers with whom they can interact, seek advice from, share responsibility for individual children and young people, and who act as a support network.

The skill set required of carers and workers living and working alongside children and young people with such complex needs is vast and needs to be tailored to the specific needs of each child. The children and young people are dependent on workers and carers whom they trust, who have the skills to enable them to grow and develop, and who offer them hope and a future. The carers and workers are central to the ethos, care, and well-being of children and young people for whom they have responsibility, and the creation of a therapeutic milieu which is child-centred. Specifically, through the creation of an 'environment designed to enhance or provide treatment, education, socialisation, support and protection to children and youth with identified mental health or behavioural needs in partnership with

DOI: 10.4324/9781032657592-6

their families and in collaboration with a full spectrum of community-based formal and informal helping resources' (Whittaker et al., 2014: 24).

Fundamentally, an organisation, whether a residential children's home, a school, or an international company, is only as good as its staff. Consequently, the way the organisation or group setting cares for, respects, values, and develops its workers, carers, and managers is critical. Any claims in terms of ethos, culture, and values that an organisation makes must be evidenced in its day-to-day practice not only for the children and young people in its care but the experience of the staff that supports them. Workers and carers who are well-trained and part of a community of practice with a child-centred philosophy, who share their knowledge, insight, and understanding of the mindset of the abused child or young person in the care system, are critical.

When foster carers and therapeutic residential home workers take on the day-to-day responsibility of children and young people, there are two domains that they are responsible for, namely, the psychological and emotional well-being of the young person, and their physical care and well-being. Although these can be viewed and addressed separately, for infants, children, and young people who have experienced profound trauma, they are often interrelated, with one having an impact on the other. As a consequence, a range of other mental and physical health services have an important part to play in the extended care of these children and young people. These will range from specialist teachers in schools, opticians, dentists and dental hygienists, hearing, speech, and language therapists, play therapists, physiotherapists, psychotherapists, and mental health services who specialise in eating disorders, depression, self-harm, anger management, conduct disorders and suicidal ideation. Ingram and Robson (2018: 189) highlight the understanding and expertise required when counselling in such cases, observing that the physical, emotional and cognitive functioning of young people who have experienced trauma is rarely synchronised and who whilst physically mature, may present as emotionally and cognitively under developed. Additionally, staff will also have close contact with medical and health specialists where children and young people need periods of stay in hospital with conditions such as bowel or bladder problems, sickle cell disease, physical disabilities, or on-going chronic health conditions.

These specialists will see children and young people intermittently, or on a 'need' basis in comparison to foster carers and workers and carers in therapeutic residential children's home who live alongside the children and young people, nevertheless it is the responsibility of the foster carer or the residential home to oversee and maintain these interventions ensuring and managing the child's continuity of good health and long-term care.

This wrap-around care and responsibility is taken as a given in the care of children and young people with profound trauma; however, the core roles of foster carers and workers in therapeutic residential children's homes need to be examined in more detail. The six key areas presented here are used to examine the role and practice of this group of carers and workers and to address issues of professional confidence, sustainability, vicarious trauma, and the danger of emotional burnout.

The aim is to enable carers and workers to develop self-reflective practice, allowing them to examine the issues which may impact their mental well-being, resilience, and critically, their capacity to support and work with children and young people, effectively.

  i The context: childminders or mental health care professionals?
  ii The residential home as a learning organisation
  iii The residential care worker as a reflective practitioner
  iv Carers and workers belief and ability to transform lives
  v Recognising and managing vicarious trauma
  vi Developing a therapeutic setting: implications for practice

The context: childminders or mental health care professionals?

Workers and carers are professionals who work and care on a daily basis with the most traumatised and vulnerable group of children and young people. Their role is not simply to ensure their physical care and safety but to provide stability, supportive relationships, and work therapeutically with this group of young people to enable the slow process of emotional development and growth. Children and young people whose early experiences have been dominated by abuse, neglect, and violence live lives shaped by the impact of this trauma. These experiences are so profound that they can arrest the normal development of the child's sense of self, their emotional, cognitive, and behavioural development, and their ability to form relationships, ultimately distorting their understanding of the world and viewing the outside world as hostile and overwhelming. Inevitably, their experiences will shape their relationships with the adults who care and work with them. Abused children suffer alone and grow up without anyone to help them make sense of what is happening to them. Trust has been betrayed and the child grows up unable to trust anyone (Farnfield and Stokowy, 2014: 65). Further, where early trauma has been profound, the mind distorts or omits experiences and information in order to psychologically deal with unbearable anxiety (Bowlby, 1980 'defensive exclusion').

In light of this, it is important that carers and workers who live alongside and care for children and young people who have experienced profound trauma understand the impact of trauma in disrupting the key developmental elements of infancy that provide the foundation for the child's evolving sense of self and their relationships with others. These include developing a primary attachment relationship, forming internal working models of self, others, and the world, and learning to regulate affect (feelings, immediate emotions, and longer-term mood). The infant or young child may develop a range of maladaptive behaviours which enable them to survive in a hostile world which they carry through into childhood and adolescence. The carer or worker must have the training and insight to recognise these maladaptive behaviours for what they are, and what they say about the child's inner world and their sense of self.

To cope, the child/young person may develop defence mechanisms to help them survive and manage living in the world. However, these defence mechanisms hide and repress feelings of rage, extreme anxiety and helplessness, feelings, and emotions, which they cannot think about or communicate to others but are expressed in the high-risk behaviours and high levels of harm towards themselves and others. These behaviours cannot be managed in a reactive way but require an understanding of the impact of the trauma on the child/young person, to peel back the layers, to find a starting point to help the child/young person to begin the process of beginning to find a way to grow through the trauma of the early experience and the maladaptive behaviour strategies of survival. High-quality and supportive caregiving relationships between workers and young people lie at the basis of enabling the child/young person to re-engage with their sense of self and live in the outside world with a degree of independence and resilience rather than being drawn into a life defined by the juvenile justice system.

Workers' and carers' skills, professionalism, and contribution to society, however, are often not recognised by other care professionals, the public, and the outside world, including local authority and national policymakers. This is reflected in their salary, status, and training, where few staff come into the profession with relevant qualifications and experience. This, and how this sector is viewed by the outside world, has an impact on the way workers and carers perceive themselves as professionals.

Concerns about personal confidence, expertise, and the professional recognition of children's residential home care workers were raised by Smith and Carroll (2015). Their study identified four critical areas, namely, workers' confidence and a perception of being undervalued by other mental health professionals which were reflected in their status and salaries; their ability to articulate their role and expertise; the fluidity and responsiveness required of them when working with young people with complex emotional and behavioural needs; and their need for specialist knowledge and additional training.

The need for a more flexible approach to qualifications and training was reinforced by White et al. (2015: 80), who recommended a range of entry points including access courses, apprenticeships, diploma, and degree courses. A key point, given issues of staffing capacity, was the importance of creating a system that enabled individuals who were recognised as having a real ability and expertise when working with this group of young people but did not have an academic background or ability to study based on the current models on offer, to develop and succeed. The qualities identified as essential included an ability to care, a commitment and passion for the job, emotional maturity, intelligence, and resilience, in addition to core knowledge and practice skills (White et al., 2015: 7–8).

The issue of staffing capacity and the effect of COVID on both young people and providers were highlighted by Ofsted (2022a) in their report on children's social care. They noted the negative impact on both workers and children because providers, through no fault of their own, were unable to ensure appropriate placements and provision for children and young people who were close to areas where they had family, in areas which they were familiar with, and went to school.

Of concern was that many residential care workers, who were typically on low salaries, left the profession for jobs with higher pay and a better work-life balance, citing the demanding nature of care work, the responsibility of the role, and the need to work shifts. Ofsted (2022a) reported that the turnover and vacancy rates are unacceptably high and that at any one time around 10% of children's homes do not have a registered manager in place. Critically, they found that many providers were struggling to recruit and employ registered managers, giving rise to the number of children's homes with a vacant manager post.

The residential home as a learning organisation

Both individual children's residential homes and providers carry a wealth of knowledge built on years of experience derived from working with children and young people whose lives are characterised by trauma and chaos. Often, pockets of expert practice are held by individuals, but because of the pressures within the system, time is not available to share this knowledge between workers in individual homes or across homes managed by individual providers. Individual care workers, whether because of opportunity, professional confidence, or status, may not feel that they have knowledge and experience that can be shared with other members of the team within which they work. This critical resource lies untapped, and so the 'go to' position is to call in consultants. One of the first steps is to conduct a two-stage analysis identifying strengths, weaknesses, opportunities for development, and threats (or barriers) to development (SWOT analysis). Stage 1 is carried out by the individual carer or worker and is centred on their own experience. Stage 2 requires that all the individual outcomes from Stage 1 are placed on a common template providing an overview. This then acts as a starting point for the home or provider to identify where strengths, weaknesses, opportunities for development and threats or barriers to development exist, and forms the basis for action planning. Importantly, it also identifies where expertise lies, held by individuals who can act as leads or a resource for the rest of the team.

Knowledge that is derived from experience and reflection, and that is responsive to the specific needs of learners, whether adults across a range of professions, or this particular case, children and young people who live with the legacy of trauma, is framed by experiential learning theory (Kolb, 1984; Kolb and Kolb, 2005). The theory is underpinned by a process of reflective learning (Figure 6.1) that is based on four elements: concrete experience, reflective observation, abstract conceptualisation, and active experimentation.

The advantage of this learning process is that not only can it be used effectively by the adult worker or carer, but that it can be taught too, and used by the child/young person to help them to begin to make sense of their experiences and behaviour. In this way learning and knowledge are created through the transformation of experience (Kolb and Kolb, 2005: 194). Importantly, learning and the creation of knowledge are no longer the domain of 'experts' since the technical language and concepts used by experts can be learnt and applied by practitioners in the

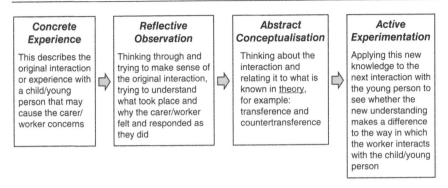

Concrete Experience	Reflective Observation	Abstract Conceptualisation	Active Experimentation
This describes the original interaction or experience with a child/young person that may cause the carer/ worker concerns	Thinking through and trying to make sense of the original interaction, trying to understand what took place and why the carer/worker felt and responded as they did	Thinking about the interaction and relating it to what is known in theory, for example: transference and countertransference	Applying this new knowledge to the next interaction with the young person to see whether the new understanding makes a difference to the way in which the worker interacts with the child/young person

Figure 6.1 Experiential learning theory – the role of reflective learning.

workplace. To ensure that this transition in culture takes place, it is useful to have an individual, who may be a consultant, who will act as a mentor, taking the team through this process of learning, before handing it over to the team themselves.

Carers and workers as reflective practitioners

Reflective practice (Schön, 1983, 1987) offers an important opportunity for carers and workers to think through, reflect on the strengths of their practice, and identify areas for development. Where this is carried out systematically, it provides residential care teams with a record, and from that, a focus to discuss both common and individual issues and to identify areas and ways forward. These ways forward can include training, mentoring, coaching, developing strategies for responding to, and managing challenging and confrontational behaviour, developing individual resilience and personal development. These ensure workers feel supported and valued and offer opportunities to address issues of mental health and burnout.

The opportunity for the individual to meet and discuss how they feel having been with specific children all day is important. This 'debriefing' enables them to learn to separate the emotions that have been projected onto them by the child/young person, and which they have taken on (*projection and transference*), in contrast to the emotions that arise within the worker in response to those projected onto them (*countertransference*). Articulating their own positive or negative emotions will give the worker an understanding of the emotional life of the child and provide an opportunity to reflect on the impact of intensive therapeutic work on a day-to-day basis. It is important to recognise that a carer or worker who has 'leaky' or semi-permeable boundaries and finds themselves responding emotionally to specific children is vulnerable to vicarious trauma.

The practice of reflection, whether as part of being supervised, end-of-day or weekly debriefing sessions with the residential home team, or recording one's own emotions, thoughts, and reflections following interactions with specific children, using the reflective log proforma in Chapter 3, is essential. This acts as a record

Daily Log: Short reflective log completed after each interaction with a child focused on identifying issues arising for the worker

Weekly Review: The reflective logs are discussed and reviewed with the manager to identify strategies for addressing the issues/ behaviours of the child and the response arising by the worker to identify strategies for management

Monthly Team Review: The aim of the monthly team review is to identify and discuss common issues and strategies that work/ examples of best practice, and also to identify whether there is a need for the agreement of a strategic approach across the team for the management of an individual child, or to bring in an external consultant to work with the team as a whole on specific areas

Figure 6.2 Workers' and carers' professional development reflection and review process.

to communicate unexpressed or repressed feelings and developing understanding about the children/young people with whom they work. It can be painful and difficult for workers to manage working with specific children whose inner world of reality is so emotionally fragile, without losing their own sense of self and a sense of confidence as competent professional. The practice of reflection offers a valuable starting point that will enable both carers and workers to develop their understanding of therapeutic practice (Figure 6.2).

Another useful way of developing the process of reflective practice is using a question-based approach (set out in Table 6.1). This model uses questions drawn directly from the experience of workers, which are related to underlying concepts and theory, examining what this means for the worker in practice. This contrasts to the more usual practice where theory is presented first, and the worker required to think about what it means in their day-to-day practice.

Carers and workers belief and ability to transform lives

Agency within a profession, namely, the capacity to take control of and shape their environment, occurs in two forms: external and internal. Externally, it is manifested by a wider society and reflects the esteem and respect with which a profession and the individuals within it are held, and the value placed on the role that they carry out. It is ultimately evidenced in whether society listens to them, the value placed on them in the form of salaries, opportunities for progression within their field, the ability to create standards of practice, and the recognition by allied professional bodies within the wider field within which they exist.

Internally, it is manifested by individuals within the profession. Carers and workers must have a sense of agency (Bandura, 2006), a self-belief that they are

Table 6.1 The role of reflection in developing the professional skills of workers and carers

Questions and concepts	What do we understand by this?	What does this mean for the worker?
Q: I know this is important, but how do I show the child/young person that I do think of them (hold them in my mind), when we are not together, for example, when the child/young person is at school? **Underlying concept: Being held in mind**	Being 'held in mind' describes the fundamental experience of the mother-child bonding experience. It describes the emotional attunement and empathy towards the infant by the mother (primary maternal preoccupation), which enables the infant's transition into the autonomy of being a separate person (Winnicott, 1960). Children and young people who have experienced early neglect and trauma are often deprived of the emotional experience of being held in the mind by a carer who is attuned to their needs and emotions.	The task of the worker or carer here is to replicate this emotional bonding so that the child/young person feels that the person caring for them constantly thinks about them and their needs, even when not present in the same room with the child/young person. The worker must respond, by communicating (verbally and non-verbally), that they are 'in tune' with the emotional needs of the child/young person, and that they are aware of and understand the depth of the child's anxiety.
Q: Why does 'that' child/young person make me feel so angry, drained, and a failure? **Underlying concept: Transference and countertransference**	Transference is the process whereby a child displaces onto the worker or carer feelings and ideas which originate from previous figures in child's life. The child then perceives the worker as though they were the original attacking person, which leads to destructive or self-destructive behaviour, mirroring the intensity of their emotions.	The role of reflection is of key importance here in enabling the worker to separate what belongs to the child/young person and what belongs to themselves. The worker must recognise the behaviours and emotions for what they are. They arise out of the child's life and experiences and they do not 'belong' to the worker and should be recognised as such.

(Continued)

Table 6.1 (Continued)

Questions and concepts	What do we understand by this?	What does this mean for the worker?
	In a fragile-integrated child, transference may occur at the point when the child or young person begins to feel a person with their own sense of self. Countertransference is where the worker takes on the displaced or projected emotions and behaviours, believing them to be their own.	Countertransference: the danger is that if the worker is unaware of what is happening, they may respond personally to the intensity of emotions that projected onto them by the child because these tap into unresolved experiences and anxieties in their own life. An understanding of projection is critical since without understanding and insight, the worker is vulnerable to projecting their own unexpressed and unbearable feelings onto the child in response to what the child has projected onto them. It is unlikely that carers or workers in any setting will have the opportunity to undergo personal therapy that will enable them to reflect on issues related to their own childhood and adult experiences. As a consequence, they may be vulnerable to experiencing transference, countertransference and, 'leaky' semi-permeable boundaries which impact their interaction with the children and young people in their care.

(Continued)

Table 6.1 (Continued)

Questions and concepts	What do we understand by this?	What does this mean for the worker?
Q: I don't understand what's going on; it's like these two children have become identical twins but where one dominates the other, and the dominated one has no sense of self or independence? Q: What lies beneath the need for two children to merge? **Underlying concept: Enmeshed attachment**	This term is used to describe a situation where the boundaries between two children have become blurred, so that one child allows the needs and wants of the other child to dominate over their own, thereby losing their own sense of individual identity and autonomy. It is important to differentiate between closeness and enmeshment: closeness refers to emotional intimacy and caregiving, whereas enmeshment involves a lack of a 'self-other separation' so that one child's thoughts and feelings are merged with those of the other.	If this is the case, physical and emotional boundaries between the two children need to be reinstated so that each recognises themselves as separate individuals. However, this does not address the underlying reason for the merging to have taken place. It is only when this is understood that work to address the separation can take place. Think about: Does the more vulnerable child seek a merger to provide them with security and a sense of self, and does merger satisfy the dominant child's need for power and control? What can I learn from reviewing the child's family history – were they raised in an enmeshed family?
Q: How can I help the child/young person to communicate and relate to their fears and anxieties when they don't or can't speak to me about how they feel? **Underlying concept: The use of transitional objects**	Transitional play using cloth, a toy, or blanket provides the child with a sense of protection from the outside world. The child can use the transitional object as a bridge, helping them to move forward to the use of symbolism in their play stories, drawing, and music.	Awareness of the importance of transitional objects for some children, which act to connect the child/young person's inner world with the outer world, providing a 'stepping stone' for moving forward, for example, to symbolic play. The use of a 'transitional object' supports the child engaged in the perpetual human task of keeping inner and outer reality separate yet 'interrelated' (Winnicott, 1971: 2).

(Continued)

Table 6.1 (Continued)

Questions and concepts	What do we understand by this?	What does this mean for the worker?
Q: I thought the child/ young person was making really good progress, but now they have completely regressed. It seems to be one step forward and two steps back at the moment. What can I do? 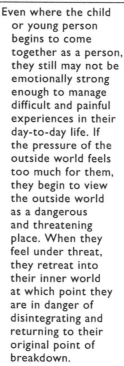 **Underlying concept: Disintegration**	Even where the child or young person begins to come together as a person, they still may not be emotionally strong enough to manage difficult and painful experiences in their day-to-day life. If the pressure of the outside world feels too much for them, they begin to view the outside world as a dangerous and threatening place. When they feel under threat, they retreat into their inner world at which point they are in danger of disintegrating and returning to their original point of breakdown.	Workers should respond sensitively and thoughtfully to the child/young person, helping them not to give up. The child/young person should feel that they are emotionally contained during a period where they feel vulnerable and under threat. It is important to recognise that an episode of disintegration is not a step backward, but instead part of a process that will lead to a 're-coming together' to form a new starting point from which the child/young person can move forward.
Q: I don't seem to be able to communicate with this child – what can I do?	The key question here is: What do we understand by communication? What form does communication take – can it be physical, symbolic, and non-verbal, as well as verbal? Does it have to be 'present', whether verbally or non-verbally, or can the lack of communication, for example, as in elective mutism, also be a form of communication?	Offer as many creative opportunities as possible for them to symbolically communicate such as drama, story writing, poetry, painting, and music. This allows the activity itself to become a mode of communication, to channel emotion and thoughts, making it easier to eventually find words to express themselves.

(Continued)

Table 6.1 (Continued)

Questions and concepts	What do we understand by this?	What does this mean for the worker?
Q: Is challenging behaviour a mode of communication? Q: Is withdrawal or the child/young person not willing or able to speak, a mode of communication? 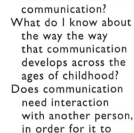 **Underlying concept: Symbolic communication**	What do I know about the various forms of communication? What do I know about the way the way that communication develops across the ages of childhood? Does communication need interaction with another person, in order for it to develop?	The child/young person needs to be aware that you are prepared to learn with them. They need opportunities for sensory play. Whatever their age, good primary play experiences that include music, play with puppets, storytelling, reading books, or writing stories with a person who they feel emotionally contained by, and who can survive their need to destroy their play (McMahon, 2009), is invaluable. The child/young person needs to have a regular time each day when they play with a specific adult who they can depend on, to use their play opportunities in ways which can help their emotional development.
Q: I thought we were getting somewhere and their behaviour is really improving, but suddenly out of the blue, they totally unravel, what's going on? Q: Am I reactive or proactive in response to the child/young person's outbursts? Q: Have I noticed any patterns in terms of what precedes the behaviour escalating, e.g., frustration, tiredness, at points of transition, and if so, am I able to ask them if there is anything that I can do to help them?	Children who act out their pain rather than locking it down are often diagnosed with 'oppositional defiant behaviour', 'attachment disorder', or 'conduct disorder'. But these labels ignore the fact that rage and withdrawal are only facets of a whole range of desperate attempts at survival. Trying to control a child's behaviour while failing to address the underlying issue, namely, the abuse that has taken place, leads to treatments that are ineffective at best and harmful at worst (Van der Kolk, 2014: 338).	The child or young person needs one-to-one help during their emotional loss of control. They need to know that they have not been emotionally rejected but are 'held in mind' by their key worker or carer. It is important to make sure that the child knows that you are aware of this anxiety. Create as many opportunities as possible for the child to communicate at a non-verbal and symbolic level rather than verbally. Acting out can be a breakdown of communication, which needs to be understood and addressed symbolically.

(Continued)

Table 6.1 (Continued)

Questions and concepts	What do we understand by this?	What does this mean for the worker?
Q: Does the team have a common strategy for handling with children/ young people whose behaviour escalates and they lose control of themselves? **Underlying concept: Conduct disorder: challenging behaviour as a form of communication**	The child/young person's expression of their anger, panic, and rage is out of their control and is deep-seated. These emotions belong to experiences of trauma which cannot be worked through or thought about, and which emerge to overwhelm them. At this point, they need to feel that they are 'emotionally contained' rather than punished or rejected actions, which feed into their earlier trauma.	Smith and Carroll (2015) reported that there was a perceived skill deficit, claiming a lack of consensus about the knowledge, practical advice, and strategies that residential workers have or ought to have, about how to manage the complex behavioural problems presented by the young people for whom they cared.
Q: Can I recognise the symptoms of vicarious trauma? *Q: What can we as a team do to address this?* **Underlying concepts:** • **Workers and carers experiencing vicarious trauma** • **Post-traumatic stress disorder (PTSD) in children and young people**	Vicarious trauma can manifest itself where workers are overwhelmed with the powerful impact of children living with post-traumatic stress disorder (PTSD). The symptoms of vicarious trauma can range from rage, guilt, helplessness, preoccupation with a child/young person's trauma out of work, to actively avoiding contact with a specific child/young person (refer to section 'Recognising and managing vicarious trauma').	Living alongside children and young people with PTSD is difficult, and where there is insufficient support for staff, and staff themselves have 'leaky' boundaries, there is a danger of workers experiencing vicarious trauma (refer to section 'Recognising and managing vicarious trauma').

(Continued)

Table 6.1 (Continued)

Questions and concepts	What do we understand by this?	What does this mean for the worker?
	PTSD in children and young people can manifest itself in psychological and physical problems that can develop in response to threatening and distressing experiences, such as physical, sexual, or emotional abuse. Typical features of PTSD include repeated and intrusive distressing memories that can cause a feeling of 'reliving or re-experiencing' the trauma, emotional detachment and social withdrawal, avoidance of reminders and sleep disturbance (NHS, 2023)	The danger here for the worker who is overloaded and overwhelmed with sharing the pain of the children/young people for whom they are responsible is the likelihood of experiencing vicarious trauma. Supporting the mental health of workers to avoid burnout is critical.
Q: I have always been confident in working around young people, but my new line manager constantly undermines me and makes me feel like I don't know what I'm doing. They keep cutting me off when I try to say anything or speak up in meetings ... I am beginning to believe that I am ineffective, and I have lost all confidence in my ability to make decisions, and I have noticed changes in the way my colleagues are starting to behave towards me. What's going on?	Identification with the aggressor (Freud, 1966) describes a defence mechanism where the lines are blurred between 'who projects and who receives' and how this then impacts of the self-identity of the person at the receiving end (the weaker person), who identifies with the aggressor (the stronger person) as a means of survival.	Working with traumatised children who present with challenging behaviours is not the only thing that can lead to emotional burnout. It is important recognise that **toxic** working environments can lead to burnout, so that the individual is torn between a love of their work with children and young people, and a hatred for the culture or specific people one works with who undermine, bully, and show little respect but carry power.

(Continued)

Table 6.1 (Continued)

Questions and concepts	What do we understand by this?	What does this mean for the worker?
Underlying concept: Identification with the aggressor (in this case the line manager) by colleagues	It is important to periodically look at our behaviour to decide whether we in fact moulding our behaviour to conform to others' projections. This vulnerability might come about for a number of reasons including exhaustion and burnout, wanting to please another individual, insecurity, or wanting to keep your job.	This is the antithesis of a supportive, caring community of practice Lave and Wenger (1991) where colleagues are valued and make it a pleasure to come to work.

able to make a difference through their work, to transform lives. Where carers and workers feel powerless either in their inability to work positively with the children and young children for whom they are responsible, or feel overwhelmed and disenfranchised by the system within which they work, they will be susceptible to burnout and leaving the profession. Critically, their sense of agency and self-efficacy (Bandura, 1977), or in contrast, powerlessness, whether that experienced by individual carers or workers or the care setting itself, will inevitably be transmitted unconsciously and experienced by the children or young people themselves. Where a sense of the powerlessness of the adults in charge, is coupled with the young person's sense of helplessness and abandonment, the impact is profound.

In contrast, where carers and workers have a sense of agency, and self-efficacy, they are able to transmit a sense of hope and that the future 'is possible'. Self-efficacy is important for children and young people who carry with them the legacy of early trauma and where they experience heightened emotional arousal and are unable to cope with what they see as threatening situations. Fear reactions generate anticipation of fear-provoking thoughts, memories of trauma, and powerlessness (Bandura, 1977: 198). Self-efficacy is critical for children and young people who live with the legacy of profound trauma because it is not simply a question of confidence, but about their belief in their ability to exercise control over their own functioning, their vulnerability, and events that affect their lives. The role of carers and workers is critical.

For children and young people in the care system where there is limited or no access to kinship family, the home, the carers and workers, and the children and young people within it become a surrogate family within which the child or young person can grow and develop emotionally with a stronger sense of self, agency, and self-efficacy.

A fundamental belief of carers and workers directly involved in the therapeutic day-to-day lives of children and young people should be that they have the capacity to transform lives. This belief is evidenced not only in their personal beliefs, but through:

- 'In-house' training, continuing professional, and personal development
- Being part of a community of practice which shares common values and ethos about the value of therapeutic practice
- Carers and workers being able to respond confidently to the question: How do we prepare young people for life beyond the foster or residential home?

Carers and workers must recognise that they hold a very particular role in enabling children and young children to develop independence, especially where they have lived in care settings where there is little opportunity to exercise independence and where decisions have been made for them.

Educating a young person for life beyond the foster home or residential home setting requires a specialist skill set and access to a wider curriculum that is focused on enabling children and young people to manage transitions ranging from childhood into adolescence and adolescence into independence and young adulthood as care leavers. This group of young adults needs to manage life and decision-making in the complex world of adult life beyond foster care and residential children's homes. The transition from a state of dependency experienced in care to living independently, is profound and life changing. Independent living involves finding appropriate supported accommodation, decisions about continuing education, managing money, cooking, caring for themselves and their health, moving into the world of work through apprenticeships and working, developing supportive and positive relationships, sexual, and mental health, dealing with anxiety, and managing their own safety both physically and online, especially since the NSPCC report significant increases in online peer-on-peer abuse and a growing prevalence in sexual exploitation of young people (NSPCC, 2021). Practical exercises and modelling of responses to behaviour enable both children and young people to begin the process of developing confidence, self-efficacy, and independence.

As part of this, it is important to review personal, social, health, and economic (PSHE) education and provision for children and young people within the therapeutic care setting. Although a PSHE curriculum will be carried out in both primary and secondary schools, given the topics covered, the emphasis and focus for a child or young person who has experienced profound trauma needs to be thought through and planned carefully. Their trauma may originate with experiences of sexual, emotional, and physical abuse, domestic violence, neglect, and broken family relationships in a home where drugs, alcohol, and mental illness define the adults, and where only one parent was present, or was in prison. Issues of safeguarding and an understanding of the child or young person's vulnerability are paramount.

The Department for Education (DfE, 2015: 4) defines PSHE as a planned pro-gramme of school-based learning opportunities and experiences that deal with the real-life issues children and young people face as they grow up, and comprises two strands: personal well-being and economic well-being:

- The personal well-being strand can cover issues such as sex and relationships education, drug and alcohol education, emotional health and well-being, diet and healthy lifestyle, and safety education.
- The economic well-being strand can cover issues such as careers guidance and education, work-related learning, enterprise education, and financial capability.

These are critical areas of knowledge that a young person leaving the care system at the age of 18 must have, since on leaving their foster placement or residential children's home, they are required to live independently and safely, without access the safety net of familiar carers or workers. Even though they are required to have a designated personal advisor and pathway plan, essentially, they will need to make the transition from being dependent to being independent, on their own.

The key questions that must be asked by the care setting in reviewing personal, social, health and economic (PSHE) provision are: What preparation exists within the setting to support the young person's transition from care to living independently? What specific areas are covered in terms of PSHE, and importantly, how are they covered, and how effectively have they been taught given the background and experiences of the children and young people? Are there areas which have not been covered, and if so, what will be done to address these? It is important that carers and workers should acknowledge that they do not shoulder the total respon-sibility for these young lives that are locked into the care system, but that schools, for example, have safeguarding rules in place, and through the specialist skills and curriculum that schools offer are able to complement and reinforce emotional sup-port, life skills, personal and social skills, and the capacity to learn.

Good teaching in schools that are child-centred, that have a positive ethos and place value on the relationships between staff and children, foster stability, learn-ing, and a place of belonging, is central to addressing the underachievement of children in care. The 2023 report 'Findings from the big ask: Children in care' commissioned by the Children's Commissioner (CCo) and Coram on the views of young people in care reported that children experienced

> *being underestimated or judged, particularly by adults, friends, and members of the community, based on their current situation. Children in care said they had been told that they couldn't achieve or that they weren't good enough to succeed or follow their dreams later in life. Many children in this sample attributed this to their current living or financial situation, as it was different from many other children they knew.*

(2023: 14)

Developing a positive partnership with primary and secondary schools, not only advantages the child or young person, but offers insight and new ways of learning for the carer or worker themselves through being part of different community, which also offers a point of reference into the child's life. Additionally, through discussing the school curriculum with the school, issues such underachievement, bullying, drugs education, online pornography, and child exploitation can be addressed within a whole school context rather than it being the sole responsibility of the carer or worker.

Recognising and managing vicarious trauma

The effect on workers and carers living alongside children and young people whose lives have been defined by trauma cannot be underestimated. They have to psychologically manage the conflicting views that are evidenced in their daily experience, namely, the reality of violence within the family, as against the cultural ideal that family is a safe place. The young people that foster carers and workers in residential settings care for live with the impact of trauma, loss, violence, fear, poverty, depression, hopelessness, and helplessness and a wide range of other physical and mental health issues (CETC, 2019: 35). Inevitably, carers and residential workers who care for these children and young people on a daily basis are vulnerable to vicarious trauma (Bloom, 2003), in the form of stress, emotional burnout, and the development of secondary traumatic stress leading to high staff turnover (The Australian Centre for Excellence in Therapeutic Care (CETC), 2019). The way that residential homes care, train, and develop their workers to ensure their mental health, psychological boundaries, and resilience is critical.

Unique settings, such as working in secure settings or with unaccompanied asylum-seeking children and young people, are difficult and complex. These are stressful environments for workers who are trying to engage meaningfully with young people whilst maintaining their own personal and professional barriers to avoid engaging in transference and countertransference, and ultimately, burnout.

Given the extreme histories of child/young people who are cared for by carers and workers, the potential of experiencing vicarious trauma, which may build up over time of working with children/young people who live with post-traumatic stress, is inevitable. Ireland et al. (2022: 43) cited experiences including

> witnessing or being a victim of physical and sexual aggression, witnessing self-injury or suicidal behaviour, and reading about neglect, abuse, self-injury, suicidal behaviour, and physical and sexual aggression from residents' histories.

The rise of feelings of ineffective coping, helplessness, and finding it difficult to cut off from events that happen during the day gives rise to two questions:

i. *How do we recognise vicarious trauma?*

ii. *What can we do to protect the emotional and physical health of carers and workers to prevent burnout?*

i. The British Medical Association (BMA) (2020) lists the following cognitive and emotional characteristics as symptoms of vicarious trauma:

- Experiencing lingering feelings of anger, rage, and sadness about patient's victimisation
- Becoming overly involved emotionally with the patient
- Experiencing bystander guilt, shame, and feelings of self-doubt
- Being preoccupied with thoughts of patients outside of the work situation
- Over-identification with the patient (having horror and rescue fantasies)
- Loss of hope, pessimism, and cynicism
- Distancing, numbing, detachment, cutting patients off, staying busy. Avoiding listening to client's story of traumatic experiences
- Difficulty in maintaining professional boundaries with the client

Unlike a psychiatrist, who may have intermittent interaction with an individual child, carers and workers are in constant daily contact with the same traumatised children. The experiences of these children and young people have been so extreme that it impacts their sense of self, confidence, their ability to communicate, to interact with others, their behaviour, and who critically, may be a danger to themselves and to others. The complexity of the children's experiences may be further compounded by the children having experienced and internalised vicarious family trauma and its impact on the way that they had been parented.

The tension, that is central to managing vicarious trauma, is essentially that of workload and the extent of the exposure to traumatised and abused children and young people, versus the support practices that are available to the worker by the organisation. Méndez-Fernández et al. (2022: 1105) reported that,

> Excessive workload and trauma caseload were associated with lower levels of recovery experiences and organisational support, making the rise of vicarious trauma more likely. On another hand, recovery practices and organisational support protected individuals from vicarious trauma and fostered vicarious resilience, both directly and indirectly, buffering the influence of workload and trauma caseload on vicarious trauma and vicarious resilience.

ii. *The question that then needs to be addressed is what strategies and support mechanisms can be put into place in the workplace to protect the emotional and physical health of workers to prevent burnout?*

Given issues of staffing, workload, and the complexity of living alongside children and young people with complex trauma, it is essential that the workplace is experienced as offering psychological safety in that workers feel listened to, supported, and valued, and where there are opportunities to talk, raise issues about their practice without risk or judgement. Opportunities to talk about practice must be built into a daily and weekly system, which allows individual issues to be raised immediately and then shared with the rest of the team, to allow shared discussion and the development of understanding to take place. There should not be a distance between workers, team leaders, and managers, or situations where individuals are afraid to speak out, and feel that things must be bottled up, or that they have no one else to rely on and must cope with things on their own. Staff are vulnerable to symptoms of vicarious trauma where they feel overwhelmed, tired, isolated and feel that the child/young person's care and even survival is dependent on them, and critically where staff themselves carry early or repressed trauma in their backgrounds. Processes should be put in place to ensure that managers are alert for symptoms of vicarious trauma in their staff and themselves. Good social support is key, and knowledge of theory, on-going training, the development of competence in practice strategies and techniques, and awareness of the potential of vicarious traumatization and the need to take deliberate steps to minimize the impact, serve as protective factors (Bloom, 2003: 459).

An important and overlooked source of stress is that of the setting itself. What happens if the worker finds themselves in a situation where the stress and powerlessness they experience have nothing to do with the traumatised children and young people that they work with, but come from the workplace itself? A setting, whether a social care system, residential children's home, a secure setting within the juvenile justice system or a group working with unaccompanied asylum-seeking children, can have the characteristics of a dysfunctional family. Consequently the stress experienced by the worker in their workplace far exceeds that generated through working with traumatised children and young people.

Bloom (2003: 466) highlights the following characteristics common to dysfunctional workplaces:

- An ongoing culture of crisis, where long-term and preventive solutions are not formulated because all time and resources are spent on 'putting out fires'
- The replacement of democratic processes with authoritarian decision-making and rigid hierarchies
- A culture of shaming, blaming, and judgmentalism
- Maintenance of order through isolation, splitting, overcontrol, manipulation, and deceitful practices, leading to mistrust and avoidance
- Little humour with positive emotions discouraged and negative emotions tolerated or encouraged
- Eventual development of a culture of toughness and meanness or actual violence
- Denial that any real problems exist
- A high degree of hypocrisy in daily functioning
- Active discouragement of confronting reality

The quality and nature of leadership are fundamental to the workplace as is the way the workers and carers experience the ethos, values, and practice of a setting. Inevitably, a supportive, collegiate workplace that is inclusive, that develops its staff and functions as a community of practice (Lave and Wenger, 1991) will have a strong record of staff retention. In contrast, a setting that is unsupportive, punitive, and that does not recognise or develop its staff, given that staff are poorly paid, will be unable to hold on to staff. The knock-on effect on the children and young people being cared for is profound. They will not be given the opportunity to develop long-term stable relationships with carers and workers because of the high turnover of staff. Critically, they will sense the dysfunctional relationships and 'atmosphere' of the setting because this will be one that, given their own backgrounds of profound trauma and dysfunctional families and relationships, they are very familiar with.

Developing a therapeutic setting: implications for practice

Two key elements are examined here: the characteristics of a therapeutic setting and the personal and professional development of staff to support this.

An effective therapeutic setting is characterised by a holistic culture, one that not only recognises and addresses the needs of the children and young people who live in the residential children's home, but one that also cares, supports, and develops the workers themselves. The fundamental basis for a therapeutic children's residential home is a recognition that the children in care live with the legacy of profound trauma, and that staff share a common understanding about how to address their needs and emotions, enabling them to develop and grow.

It is a concern that there is no consensus about the definition of a therapeutic setting, and importantly, how therapeutic care should be translated into day-to-day practice. The key task then is to address this, ensuring that the manager and staff collectively define what they understand by a therapeutic culture, the underlying theory, philosophy, values, and practice that characterises this, and to identify the training needed by workers to support this. Changes in understanding and practice take time to embed, so the identification of best practice within the residential children's home is an important step, as is the identification of areas for development.

The culture of a therapeutic residential children's home should be values-driven and people-centred. The manager as a leader should have the capacity to create, live, and sustain a therapeutic milieu/setting. They should be viewed as an expert practitioner by staff and colleagues, one whose decision-making is trusted and who models best practice. The manager should demonstrate the ability to deal with complexity, messiness, ambiguity, and cognitive dissonance, with the capacity to see through problems, to get to the underlying issues and identify potential solutions with confidence (Kinchington, 2020: 15). The values, vision, and ethos of the manager themselves and the trust they are able to engender in both their colleagues and the young people for whom they care are key. Being able to articulate what the manager understands by a therapeutic residential setting, how they are able to build a culture where all staff 'buy into' this, and how they are able to embed these core values in the working practice of the residential home is essential in transforming practice. It is informed by the current understanding of trauma and its impact on the development of the child, which is translated into practice and embedded in the therapeutic care programme. It involves understanding and responding to the developmental, emotional, social, and cognitive functioning, and the development of relationships of unintegrated children and young people. There is no one-size-fits-all, but a need for individualised, tailored interactions, strategies, and responses that meet the young person's mental health and behavioural needs at any given time. The ultimate aim is to enable a stronger and more integrated sense of self and functioning of the child/young person, where they are able to communicate and accept the consequences of their actions, behaviour, and their emotions.

Claiming effectiveness and improvement in the lives of children, who have experienced profound trauma to the extent that it has arrested their emotional, psychological, and behavioural development, is very difficult; irrespective of how much monitoring and evaluation take place, since there is no single starting point that is common to all children. Change is not a linear trajectory, constantly moving forward, and when change does occur, it may be subtle and take many years to become internalised by the child/young person. The impact of the trauma on the child's/young person's development may be characterised by progress, then disintegration, followed by slow evolution, but critically always from a new starting point. It is important to recognise that this evolution may be unpredictable may be dependent on stable relationships with key workers, the child's age, and the therapeutic culture of the home. Changes may be tiny, but significant in terms of the child's development, and when viewed from a longitudinal perspective and compared to the child's starting point on entry to the residential home. This type of 'ipsative' assessment offers a measure of the child/young person's progress against themselves rather than against outside measures, or compared to other children. For example, the home may be able to show that a child was originally assessed as being in a frozen state of unintegration on their entry to the home, but over a three-year period of structured support by the team, has now achieved a sufficient level of emotional integration to enable them to consider being fostered.

However, where does this leave foster carers, who work individually outside the support of a team setting? Leslie et al. (2005) report that there is limited use of foster parents as 'therapeutic agents'. They note that foster parents are not equipped to manage children with developmental and/or behavioural needs and highlight the need to train specialised foster parents who can offer therapeutic foster care for children who are medically fragile, developmentally disabled, or emotionally disturbed.

Developing a positive professional identity: self-care is critical when working with such complex young people and runs alongside professional competence. It ranges from taking time to eat properly, spending time on looking after yourself, managing your work-life balance with time spent on family, friends, and relationships, and getting enough sleep. Self-care is essential for the worker and an important part of professional practice that helps to address issues of emotional exhaustion and to avoid dangers such as compassion fatigue in a high-stress field (Figley, 2002). The teaching for self-care within social work training courses (Lewis and King, 2019) has advocated an important part of ensuring resilience in professionalism.

Professional growth through training

Personal and professional development of carers, workers, and managers is intrinsic to the development and maintenance of a therapeutic culture whether residential or individual. In terms of opportunity, an individual foster carer living alongside a child who has experienced profound trauma may only have access to periodic training and support, and in some cases, feel isolated rather than part of a supportive team. They may not have colleagues who will offer emotional support, raise concerns of vicarious trauma or to bounce ideas off, in real time.

In contrast, workers and carers who are part of therapeutic children's residential home have the advantage of being part of a community of practice in which the in-house culture of a therapeutic community, where the potential for developing personal and professional self-confidence and status, is offered. Importantly, additional elements available through a programme of professional development include the development of a positive professional identity that develops self-confidence; professional growth through engaging in training opportunities, learning, and responsibility; and completing appropriate qualifications. National Vocational Qualifications (NVQ) Level 3 for workers and Level 5 diploma for managers are best viewed as providing a baseline for working in the profession; however, the complexity of residential settings requires professional development outside of what is offered by these qualifications. This can be provided by in-house development that is tailored to the needs of the staff arising from the issues that emerge within the setting itself such as concrete strategies to anticipate and manage extreme behaviours, self-harm, and vicarious trauma. A valuable way forward is the Accreditation of Experiential Learning. This can take the form of a structured portfolio that includes case studies, theory, and reflective accounts of practice to provide standalone accreditation that is matched against the learning outcomes and assessment criteria and certified either by a national body or the awarding university.

Although Ireland et al. (2022) advise reducing exposure to traumatic experiences, given staffing issues and the influx of complex cases that many teams have to deal with, this may be neither viable nor realistic. However, they do advocate *emotional and proactive support from others, use of effective coping, and increased knowledge and preparation for distressing events*. This offers a positive way forward. The creation of a supportive, caring professional community of workers is dependent on the quality of leadership, trust, psychological safety, and ensuring that time is made available for reflection, support, and feedback. There is a cost to mentoring and supervising workers to develop resilience and a team ethos, and that is time and prerequisite leadership skills. Putting this to one side or neglecting it because of workload can only lead to staff burnout and decisions to leave the profession. An indicator of how well a residential home was managed, according to White et al. (2015: 8), reflected in the rates of staff turnover and the stresses of the job.

Summary

The question that a setting must ask is, how well does it look after, support, and develop its carers, workers, and managers? Failing to look after staff comes at a great cost. If staff are not happy and feel unsupported in their work, they are unlikely to be able to manage the difficult task of supporting the children and young people in their care. The need for stability in the lives of children and young people with staff that they have been able to form a trusting relationship is paramount, but will be compromised if there is high staff turnover because of workload, burnout, a toxic working environment, or the low salaries on offer. The loss of experienced carers and workers, who are able to provide good consistent primary experiences where they are attuned with the child, holding them in mind, providing stability, and acting as positive role models, will diminish the life and development of the child/young person, repeating and reinforcing early experiences of abandonment and loss.

Conclusions

Christine Bradley

Over the past few years, I have been engaged and pre-occupied with writing about the development of therapeutic treatment and practice in working with seriously traumatised children and young people. The aim of this manual is to enable carers and workers as well as those responsible for running therapeutic settings to acquire a deeper insight and understanding about what it means for the child and young person when they are addressing the complexities of the work by providing the necessary tools of practice which can help deepen their insight and understanding about the work.

The intention is to help carers and workers to be responsive to the child or young person's difficult behaviour rather than reacting to it and creating further acting out in their day-to-day living, which can be very destructive both for themselves and for those around them. Without therapeutic support which will enable the child or young person to begin the slow process of growth, they will instead enter into a pattern where each placement will continually break down and their behaviour will become more difficult to manage. Consequently, the child will give up any hope of recovery from their early experiences of trauma and abuse, and the outcome for them is as damaging as were their early experiences of abuse, privation, and negativity. Understanding how carers and workers can address the needs of children and young people whose early trauma has become so overwhelming and unbearable that it cannot be thought about, is vital, and lies at the core of therapeutic care.

The assessment and therapeutic plans work together. It is not possible to be clear about good practice that meets the emotional needs of traumatised children and young people without discussing and reviewing the plan in relation to the Needs Led Assessment. This helps workers and carers to identify and focus on the primary task which needs to be followed if they are to carry out the therapeutic treatment plan successfully when working with traumatised children who have not yet been able to reach a positive emotional starting point in their day-to-day lives. As the first chapter points out, the Needs Led Assessment programme is not a new invention of practice. It first came together during the 1970s and 1980s from the pioneering work of the Mulberry Bush School and the Cotswold community, during a period when they were both focusing on deepening their understanding about the value of their work in developing well-planned and thought-through therapeutic

DOI: 10.4324/9781032657592-7

practice. This resulted in a deeper understanding of role of therapeutic work and how this helped the children and young people to start to believe that they were individuals in their own right, and importantly, who could accept personal responsibility for themselves and their behaviour.

If the level of practice is to continue supporting a therapeutic culture to evolve with different thoughts and ideas but holding onto the underlying philosophy which produced the good outcomes for children and young people previously, it is important that the Needs Led Assessment continues to evolve and align with current conceptual and analytical thinking and practice in society. It is crucial that the methodology can fit in with current thinking without losing touch with the underlying philosophy which produced good outcomes initially.

The chapter on the vocabulary and the definition of terms brings together key psychoanalytic concepts and terms which need to be understood and used by those working with the assessment and treatment plans. It is important that new carers and workers become familiar with the concepts, ideas, and terminology and use these to deepen their understanding about therapeutic practice and how it works.

The chapters on Needs Led Assessment exemplify the process, and the case studies themselves illustrate the assessment and treatment in practice, enabling carers and workers to follow the process through.

The first three case studies were completed within the past 12 months, during which we introduced the reflective logs into the assessment and treatment plan. The feedback has been excellent and has helped carers and workers to reflect on the impact of the work both on them as practitioners, and the effectiveness of the treatment programme by providing greater insight and understanding into the needs of the child or young person. The case examples that follow were based on the original model without the reflective log. It is clear that a valuable opportunity to reflect on practice was omitted and consequently, the outcomes for some of those children were not as positive as others.

The lesson for us to learn from this is that all of us must be prepared to learn from our experiences. If the outcome is not as positive as we would prefer for those for whom we are responsible, there is always room for change if we are prepared to reflect on the situation.

The essential and difficult role of carers and workers is examined in Chapter 6 and offers strategies for developing the resilience and expertise of the profession through professional development and wider recognition of the critical role they play in the lives of traumatised children and young people.

What is important about this manual is that it highlights the importance of holding onto the insight and understanding which has been acquired over many years, referring to the importance of carers and workers being able to reach the inner world of traumatised children and young people. Therapeutic practice will help traumatised children and young people to begin the process of developing a sense of self which they feel they can live with, and the capacity to communicate their fears and uncertainties to those they trust and feel secure with, rather than 'acting out' negatively and destructively when the internal and external realities they have to face becomes more bearable, and begin to integrate and come together.

After being immersed in the writing of *Trauma in Children and Young People: Reaching the Heart of the Matter* (2023) and this manual *Developing a Therapeutic Treatment Programme for Traumatised Children and Young People: A Needs Led Assessment Model*, I have come to realise that over time, eras and society changes, politically, economically, and culturally, and that it is important that we have the flexibility to adapt our thinking. However, I have also recognised that if during the change we lose touch with the underlying philosophy which has produced good outcomes previously, then we have lost everything. I hope this manual will provide practical support to current therapeutic carers and workers to integrate both aspects of the work: holding the needs of traumatised children and young people at the core of their practice and providing a well-thought-out therapeutic approach in their work.

Afterword

Judith Trowell

It is important to reflect on the importance of this manual. *Developing a Therapeutic Treatment Programme for Traumatised Children and Young People: A Needs Led Assessment Model* will enable professionals working with children and young people to use the ideas presented here by Christine together with those in the accompanying book *Trauma in Children and Young People: Reaching the Heart of the Matter* (2023).

Why now, is this so relevant and exciting? The application of these ideas is wide-reaching. They are of relevance to the NHS, Child and Adolescent Mental Health Services (CAMHS), Accident and Emergency, inpatient settings and in the community, to primary and secondary schools, pupil referral units and special schools, to our surviving youth and community services, Social Services, and the Voluntary sector as well as secure accommodation for young offenders and those working with refugees and asylum-seeking young people.

The state of children, young people, and their families in this country and internationally is such that anything that can make a difference is important and these books convey a message of hope that something can be done. In the United Kingdom, currently, we have 8200 children in care of whom 5700 are fostered. There is widespread abuse and trauma and many children are living in homes where there is domestic abuse, drug, and alcohol abuse, and where violence and fear exist for many children and young people both at home and in the streets. Professionally, we are seeing more children and young people in despair, depressed and very anxious.

These children and young people are unable to learn. Add to this the children with physical and mental disabilities, those with autism and anorexia, both of which are increasing rapidly, and the picture is pretty grim. The final blow to the sense that we have not made any progress is to hear that Rickets caused by a vitamin D deficiency has re-emerged, with many children suffering from malnutrition.

What Christine is trying to do in her writing is to urge us not to give up, not to look for a 'one size fits all' solution, whether it be practice guidelines, targets, or the use of a legal intervention. What is needed is to spend time with the child or young person to try to understand them and how they see themselves. It is time-consuming, but as Thomas Coram said after creating his Foundling Hospital, "every child deserves the best we can do".

Out of this understanding comes the possibility of finding a way to help, to enable the child or young person to develop and grow emotionally and physically. So many children say that mum or dad are so busy, some doing three jobs, and if they make it to school, there are so many children in the class and it can be difficult if one child is disruptive, so they struggle on, not finding an adult that has time for them.

Christine outlines here how this can be done. Her suggestions give hope to the child, the young person, and the professional trying to help them. The ideas will be adapted and modified, they will evolve but that is fine, they need to be alive to reach these troubled children and young people and to try and turn their lives around.

References

Argyle, M. (1988). *Bodily communication*, 2nd ed. London: Routledge

American Psychiatric Association (APA). (2013). *Diagnostic and statistical manual of mental disorders: DSM-5™*, 5th ed. American Psychiatric Publishing Inc. https://doi.org/10.1176/appi.books.9780890425596

American Psychiatric Association (APA). (2022). *Diagnostic and statistical manual of mental disorders*, 5th ed., text rev. https://doi.org/10.1176/appi.books.9780890425787

Bandura, A. (1977). Self-efficacy: Toward a unifying theory of behavioral change, *Psychological Review*, 84(2), 191–215. https://doi.org/10.1037/0033-295X.84.2.191

Bandura A. (2006). Toward a psychology of human agency, *Perspectives on Psychological Science*, 1(2):164–180. https://doi.org/10.1111/j.1745-6916.2006.00011.x

Bion, W.R. (1962). *Learning from experience*. New York, NY: Basic Books Pub Co.

Bloom, S.L. (2003). Caring for the caregiver: Avoiding and treating vicarious traumatization. In A. Giardino, E. Datner and J. Asher (Eds.), *Sexual assault, victimization across the lifespan* (pp. 459–470). Maryland Heights, MO: GW Medical Publishing.

Bowlby, J. (1969). *Attachment: Attachment and loss: Vol. 1. Loss*. New York, NY: Basic Books.

Bowlby, J. (1980). *Loss, sadness and depression: Attachment and Loss* (vol. 3). New York, NY: Basic Books.

Bradley, C. with Kinchington, F. (2018). *The inner world of traumatized children: An attachment-informed model for assessing emotional needs and treatment*. London: Jessica Kingsley Pub.

British Medical Association (BMA). (2020). *Vicarious trauma: Signs and strategies for coping*. www.bma.org.uk/advice-and-support/your-wellbeing/vicarious-trauma/vicarious-trauma-signs-and-strategies-for-coping (Accessed 24 July 2023).

Centre for Excellence in Therapeutic Care (CETC). (2019). *Introduction to the foundational training program in intensive therapeutic care manual for managers and supervisors*. Australian Childhood Foundation with Southern Cross University. Sydney: NSW.

Children's Commissioner for England (CCo) and Coram Voice. (2023). *Findings from the big ask: Children in care*. London: Children's Commissioner for England and Coram.

De Bellis, M.D. and Zisk, A.B. (2014). The biological effects of childhood trauma, *Child and Adolescent Psychiatric Clinics of North America*, 23(2), 185–222. https://doi.org/10.1016/j.chc.2014.01.002

DfE. (2015). *Personal, social, health and economic (PSHE) education: A review of impact and effective practice*. www.gov.uk

Dockar-Drysdale, B. (1990). *The provision of the primary experience: Winnicottian work with children and adolescents*. London: Free Association Books.

Di Giuseppe, M. and Perry, J.C. (2021). The hierarchy of defense mechanisms: Assessing defensive functioning with the Defense Mechanisms Rating Scales Q-Sort, *Frontiers in Psychology*, 12, 718440. https://doi.org/10.3389/fpsyg.2021.718440

Gergely, G. and Watson, J.S. (1996). The social biofeedback theory of parental affect-mirroring: The development of emotional self-awareness and self-control in infancy, *International Journal of Psychoanalysis*, 77(6), 1181–1212.

Gross, J.J. (2002). Emotion regulation: Affective, cognitive, and social consequences, *Psychophysiology*, 39, 281–291. Cambridge University Press.

Farnfield, S. and Stokowy, M. (2014). The Dynamic-Maturational Model (DMM) of attachment. In P. Holmes and S. Farnfield (Eds.), *The Routledge handbook of attachment: Theory* (pp. 49–72). Routledge/Taylor & Francis Group.

Figley, C.R. (2002) Compassion fatigue: Psychotherapists chronic lack of self-care, *Journal of Clinical Psychology: Psychotherapy in Practice*, 58(11), 1433–1441. https://doi.org/10.1002/jclp.10090

Fitzpatrick, C., Williams, P., and Coyne, D. (2016). Supporting looked after children and care leavers in the criminal justice system: emergent themes and strategies for change. Prison Service Journal, (226), 8-13. ISSN 0300-3558 https://www.crimeandjustice.org.uk

Freud, A. (1937). *The ego and the mechanisms of defence.* London: Hogarth Press and Institute of Psycho-Analysis.

Freud, A. (1966). *The ego and the mechanisms of defence.* New York, NY: International Universities.

Ingram, S. and Robson, M. (2018). Chapter 12 pp. 183–194. In M. Robson and S. Pattison (Eds.), *The handbook of counselling children and young people.* London: Sage.

Ireland, C., Keeley, S., Lewis, M. and Bowden, S. (2022). Vicarious trauma and compassion fatigue in residential care workers of traumatized children, *Abuse: An International Impact Journal*, 3, 43–54. https://doi.org/10.37576/abuse.2022.030

Kinchington, F. (2020). Empowering the school leaders of tomorrow: What lessons can we learn from the decision-making of today's school leaders? *International Journal of Leadership in Education.* https://doi.org/10.1080/13603124.2020.1829713

Kolb, D.A. (1984). *Experiential learning: Experience as the source of learning and development.* Englewood Cliffs, NJ: Prentice Hall.

Kolb, A.Y. and Kolb, D.A. (2005). Learning styles and learning spaces: Enhancing experiential learning in higher education, *Academy of Management Learning & Education*, 4(2), 193–212. http://www.jstor.org/stable/40214287

Klein, M. (1932). *The psychoanalysis of children.* The International Psycho-analytical Library, No. 22.

Klein, M. (1961). *Narrative of a child analysis: The conduct of the psychoanalysis of children as seen in the treatment of a ten year old boy* (No. 55). New York, NY: Random House.

Lave, J. and Wenger, E. (1991). *Situated learning: Legitimate peripheral participation.* Cambridge University Press. https://doi.org/10.1017/CBO9780511815355

Leslie, L. K., Gordon, J. N., Lambros, K., Premji, K., Peoples, J. and Gist, K. (2005). Addressing the developmental and mental health needs of young children in foster care, *Journal of Developmental and Behavioral Paediatrics*, 26(2), 140–151. https://doi.org/10.1097/00004703-200504000-00011

Lewis, M.L. and King, D.M. (2019). Teaching self-care: The utilization of self-care in social work practicum to prevent compassion fatigue, burnout, and vicarious trauma, *Journal of Human Behavior in the Social Environment*, 29(1), 96–106. https://doi.org/10.1080/109 11359.2018.1482482

MacAlister, J. (2022). *The independent review of children's social care – Final report. Government proposals for children's social care reform.* www.gov.uk

McMahon, L. (2009). *The handbook of play therapy and therapeutic play.* London: Routledge.

Méndez-Fernández, A.B., Aguiar-Fernández, F.J., Lombardero-Posada, X., Murcia-Álvarez, E. and González-Fernández, A. (2022). Vicariously resilient or traumatised social workers: exploring some risk and protective factors, *The British Journal of Social Work*, 52(2), 1089–1109. https://doi.org/10.1093/bjsw/bcab085

Ministry of Justice (MoJ) Prison Education Statistics 2019 – 2020 (2021) www.gov.uk

Murray, E.T., Lacey, R., Maughan, B. and Sacker, A. (2020). Association of childhood out-of-home care status with all-cause mortality up to 42-years later: Office of National Statistics Longitudinal Study, *BMC Public Health*, 20, 735. https://doi.org/10.1186/s12889-020-08867-3

Negele, A., Kaufhold, J., Kallenbach, L. and Leuzinger-Bohleber, M. (2015). Childhood trauma and its relation to chronic depression in adulthood, *Depression Research and Treatment*, 2015, 650804. https://doi.org/10.1155/2015/650804

Newman, L., Sivaratnam, C. and Komiti, A. (2015). Attachment and early brain development – Neuroprotective interventions in infant–caregiver therapy, *Translational Developmental Psychiatry*, 3, 1. https://doi.org/10.3402/tdp.v3.28647

NHS. (2023). *Improving access to psychological therapies manual (IAPT)*. London: NHS.

NICE. (2016). *Children's attachment: Quality standard QS 133*. www.nice.org.uk/guidance/qs133

NICE. (2021). *Looked-after children and young people (NG205)*. www.nice.org.uk/guidance/ng205

Ofsted. (2022a). *Children's social care 2022: recovering from the COVID-19 pandemic*. Published 27 July 2022. https://www.gov.uk/government/publications/childrens-social-care-2022-recovering-from-the-covid-19-pandemic (Accessed 23 July 2023).

Ofsted. (2022b). *Ready or not: Care leavers views of preparing to leave care*. Manchester: Ofsted. 'Ready or not': care leavers' views of preparing to leave care - GOV.UK (www.gov.uk)

Paulus, F.W., Ohmann, S., Möhler, E., Plener, P. and Popow, C. (2021). Emotional dysregulation in children and adolescents with psychiatric disorders. A narrative review, *Psychiatry*, 12, 628252. https://doi.org/10.3389/fpsyt.2021.628252

Petzold, M. and Bunzeck, N. (2022). Impaired episodic memory in PTSD patients - A meta-analysis of 47 studies, *Frontiers in Psychiatry*, 13, 909442. https://doi.org/10.3389/fpsyt.2022.909442

Rutter, M. (1981). *Maternal deprivation reassessed*. London: Penguin.

Sacker, A., Murray, E., Lacey, R. and Maughan, B. (2021). *The lifelong health and wellbeing trajectories of people who have been in care: Findings from the Looked-after Children Grown up Project, The LACGro Project*. https://doi.org/10.13140/RG.2.2.14371.58403

Schön, D.A. (1983). *The reflective practitioner: How professionals think in action*. New York, NY: Basic Books.

Schön, D.A. (1987). *Educating the reflective practitioner: Toward a new design for teaching and learning in the professions*. San Francisco, CA: Jossey-Bass Publisher.

Smith, M. and Carroll, D. (2015). Residential child care and mental health practitioners working together, *Scottish Journal of Residential Child Care*, 14(3), 6–18.

Trowell, J., Joffe, I., Campbell, J., Clemente, C., Almqvist, F., Soininen, M., Koskenranta-Aalto, U., Weintraub, S., Kolaitis, G., Tomaras, V., Anastasopoulos, D., Grayson, K., Barnes, J. and Tsiantis, J. (2007). Childhood depression: A place for psychotherapy - An outcome study comparing individual psychodynamic psychotherapy and family therapy, *European Child & Adolescent Psychiatry*, 16, 157–67. https://doi.org/10.1007/s00787-006-0584-x

Trowell, J. and Miles, G. (2011). *Childhood depression: A place for psychotherapy*. London: Karnac Books.

Van der Kolk, B. (2014). *The body keeps the score: Brain, mind, and body in the transformation of trauma*. London, UK: Penguin.

White, C., Gibb, J. and Graham, B. with Thornton, A., Hingley, S. and Ed Mortimer, E. (2015), *Training and developing staff in children's homes*. London: DfE. DFE-RR438 ISBN: 978-1-78105-450-5. www.gov.uk/government/publications/training-and-developing-staff-in-childrens-homes

Whittaker, J.W., Del Valle, J.F. and Holmes, L. (Eds.). (2014). *Therapeutic residential care with children and youth: Developing evidence-based international practice* London and Philadelphia, PA: Jessica Kingsley Publishers. ISBN 978-1-84905-792-9.

Williams, K., Papadopoulou, V. and Booth, N. (2012). *Prisoners' childhood and family backgrounds: Results from the Surveying Prisoner Crime Reduction (SPCR) longitudinal cohort study of prisoners*. Ministry of Justice Research Series 4/12 SBN: 978-1-84099-544-2, http://www.justice.gov.uk

Winnicott, D.W. (1960). Ego distortion in terms of true and false self. In D.W. Winnicott (Ed.), *The maturational processes and the facilitating environment studies in the theory of emotional development* (pp. 140–152). London: Karnac Books.

Winnicott, D.W. (1965). *The maturational processes and the facilitating environment.* Int. Psycho. Anal. Lib., Vol. 64 (1–276). London: The Hogarth Press and the Institute of Psycho-Analysis.

Winnicott, D.W. (1971). Transitional objects and transitional phenomena (Ch.1) In D. W. Winnicott (Ed.), *Playing & reality* (pp. 1–18). London: Tavistock Publications.

COPYRIGHT PERMISSION

Dear Colleagues,

As you are aware, both this manual: **Bradley, C. with Kinchington, F. (2024)** *Developing a Therapeutic Treatment Plan for Traumatised Children and Young People: A Needs Led Assessment Model,* **London: Routledge,** and the earlier book: **Bradley, C. with Kinchington, F. (2004)** *Trauma in Children and Young People: Reaching the Heart of the Matter,* **London: Routledge,** are subject to copyright restrictions, namely that,

Should you wish to use parts of specific chapters such as the Needs Led Assessment and Therapeutic Treatment Programme models from either book as part of your training and practice, you will need to apply to the Routledge Permission Team or Copyright Clearance Centre for specific permission.

1. You will need to submit your request via the Copyright Clearance Center (CCC) Marketplace permissions clearing service:

   CCC Phone: +1 (978) 646 2600
   CCC Email: info@copyright.com

   Copyright Clearance Center (CCC)
   222 Rosewood Drive
   Danvers, MA 01923
   United States

   Processing time: 3-5 business days

2. You may also make a request through the Taylor & Francis Book Permissions form including as much detail on your request as possible and send it to book-permissions@tandf.co.uk.

   Processing time: 10 business days

Index

Note: Page references in *italics* denote figures and in **bold** tables.

Printed and bound by CPI Group (UK) Ltd, Croydon, CR0 4YY

06/11/2024

01784892-0016